napa bulletin 11

Double Vision: Anthropologists at Law

Randy Frances Kandel, ed.

National Association for the Practice of Anthropology
A Unit of the American Anthropological Association

NAPA Bulletins are occasional publications of the National Association for the Practice of Anthropology, a Unit of the American Anthropological Association.

Ralph J. Bishop and Pamela Amoss
General Editors

Library of Congress Cataloging-in-Publication Data

Double vision : anthropologists at law / edited by Randy Frances Kandel
p. cm.—(NAPA bulletin : 11)
Includes bibliographical references (p.).
ISBN 0-913167-50-9 (paperbound)
1. Law and anthropology. 2. Evidence, Expert—United States.
3. Anthropologists—United States. I. Kandel, Randy F.
II. Series.
K487.A57D68 1992
347.73'067—dc20
[347.30767] 92-15054
CIP

ISBN 0-913167-50-9

Contents

Dedicated to the memory of Isabel Wright, whose exuberant commitment to anthropology in the service of justice daily defied the inevitability of death.

Preface

In important, increasingly visible ways anthropologists are acting as experts in legal cases. Anthropologists have served as consultants and expert witnesses in Native American land claims disputes, cultural rights and religious freedom cases,[1] political asylum cases (Loucky and Alvarez, this volume), civil rights and desegregation cases,[2] First Amendment and ethnic rights cases,[3] criminal trials raising cultural issues,[4] and cultural preservation,[5] government benefits,[6] and environmental matters. Anthropologists have testified both on the basis of long-term field experience with cultures and communities and about research specifically conducted for the purposes of ongoing litigation. With burgeoning cultural pluralism and ever-sharpening economic disparities in the United States, anthropological expert testimony is emerging from the chrysalis of issue-oriented litigation about indigenous and minority peoples, where anthropological expertise is well recognized, into more commonplace family, commercial, and criminal cases.

This volume is intended as a reflective yet practical guide for anthropologists working or thinking of working with lawyers and lawyers working or thinking of working with anthropologists. Two of the contributors, Randy Frances Kandel and Michael Davidson, are both anthropologists and attorneys; three, Peter Rigby, James Loucky, and Isabel Wright, are anthropologists who work closely with attorneys; and two, Peter Sevareid and Lynn Alvarez, are attorneys who work closely with anthropologists. Because the readers of NAPA Bulletins are primarily anthropologists, this volume takes somewhat of an anthropologist's eye view in rendering familiar the exotic culture of the law. But we believe attorneys may, with equal profit and pleasure, read it "in reverse" to gain insight into the exotic culture of the anthropologist.

The genesis of this volume was in two symposia. The first, held at the 1989 Annual Meeting of the American Anthropological Association, was a theoretical exploration of the "double vision" that results from superimposing anthropological and legal analysis on a single issue. The chapters in the first section, "How Lawyers and Anthropologists Think Differently," are derived from that symposium; they compare and contrast legal and anthropological reasoning and explanation. The second symposium, held at the 1990 Southwestern Anthropological Association Annual Meeting, was a practice-oriented session on attorney-anthropologist collaboration. The chapters in the second section, "Two Case Studies of Effective Anthropological Experts," are practical "how-to" studies based on the symposium. The third section, "A Legal Field Guide for the Expert Anthropologist," was written expressly for this volume.

Like other symposia-derived publications, this volume makes no claim to completeness. Two omissions deserve comment. First, no chapter deals explicitly with cases involving indigenous peoples and minority rights, which have historically formed the bulk of anthropological testimony. To the extent that this is not happenstance, the purpose is to focus on newer and lesser known practitioner pathways, in hopes of stimulating the legal use of anthropological expertise beyond the classically anthropological domains.

Second, the volume mentions little of the numerous and knotty ethical issues raised when anthropologists become consultants and witnesses in litigation. This is not because the problem is unimportant but because it is too important and complex to be given short shrift in a book devoted to other matters.

Rather, the practice-oriented chapters operate from two common assumptions. First, they assume that an anthropologist will agree to be a consultant or expert witness on behalf of a party only when there is general consistency among the anthropologist's professional and scholarly opinions on the subject of testimony, the legal position of the case party, and the anthropologist's obligations to his people beyond the context of the case. Second, they assume that an anthropologist, having accepted such work, will participate as part of a litigation team in which testimony is strategically organized and is presented with the honesty and integrity required by a court of law and by anthropology as a scholarly discipline. Where an anthropologist's honest, objective testimony is not helpful to a party, the anthropologist will not accept or will terminate the work. Similarly, where scholarly questions or concerns for one's people beyond the scope of the case will significantly interfere with the clear, concise testimony required by the case, the anthropologist will not testify.

No claim is made to the moral or political correctness of this position. We believe, however, that it is the position that is taken most often by anthropological experts, that is most often assumed by U.S. courts, and that is most consistent with the ethical guidelines promulgated by the American Anthropological Association and the National Association of Practicing Anthropologists and with the rules of evidence and discovery applicable in U.S. jurisdictions.

Notes

[1]It is in such cases that anthropological testimony has been preeminent. So many anthropologists have testified in so many cases that to mention some would necessarily be to err by omission.

[2]For example, anthropologist Robert Redfield was an expert witness in Sweatt v. Painter, 339 U.S. 629 (1950), a precursor of Brown v. Board of Education, 347 U.S. 483 (1954), holding that the education provided at an all African-American law school was not equal to that at a white law school. Reams have been written on the impact of social science on the desegregation litigation strategy and judicial decisions.

[3]For example, in Wisconsin v. Yoder, 405 U.S. 205 (1972) the United States Supreme Court upheld the right of the Amish to culturally distinct education, exempting Amish parents from the criminal penalties applied for failing to send children to the last two years of high school education. John Hoestetler was an expert witness at trial. His testimony was relied on and liberally quoted in the Supreme Court's opinion.

[4]Anthropologists have been involved in development and testifying regarding the cultural defense: using evidence of accepted cultural practice or mistreatment of a cultural or subcultural group to mitigate the nature of the offense or penalty in a criminal trial. See, e.g., People v. Kimura, No. A-091133 (Los Angeles County Superior Court filed April 24, 1985); People v. Moua (Kong) No. 315972-0 (Fresno County Superior Court Feb. 7, 1985); People v. Moua (Tou, F-9083403) (Fresno Municipal Court, 1985); People v. Aphaylath, 68 N.Y.2d 945, 510 N.Y.S.2d 83, 502 N.E.2d 998 (1986); U.S. v. Alexander and Murdock, 471 F.2d 923 (D.C. Cir. 1972), and Wright (this volume).

[5]Anthropologists play a significant role in the governmental regulatory and administrative structure of cultural and historical preservation. (See, e.g., White 1990.)

[6]Although less directly involved in litigation, anthropologists examining the relationship between contemporary United States homelessness and poverty and the bureaucratic maze of governmental benefits are playing an important role in formulating legislation and policy (De Havenon 1989–90).

I. How Lawyers and Anthropologists Think Differently

Six Differences in Assumptions and Outlook between Anthropologists and Attorneys

Randy Frances Kandel

In his justly famous but teasingly impressionistic essay "Local Knowledge: Fact and Law in Comparative Perspective," Clifford Geertz describes the similarity between anthropological and legal reasoning:

> Between the skeletonization of fact so as to narrow moral issues to the point where determinate rules can be employed to decide them (to my mind the defining feature of legal process) and the schematization of social action so that it can be construed in cultural terms (the defining feature, also to my mind, of ethnographic analysis) there is more than a passing family resemblance . . . law and ethnography are crafts of place: they work by the light of local knowledge. . . . Whatever else anthropology and jurisprudence may have in common—vagrant erudition and a fantastical air—they are alike absorbed with the artisan task of seeing broad principles in parochial facts. [1983:170–171]

What then keeps these two "distinctive manner[s] of imagining the real" (Geertz 1983:173) apart? More than an arbitrary scholasticism. Differences in implicit paradigms of thought give lawyers and anthropologists a sense of talking at cross purposes when they collaborate. Anthropologists and attorneys who intend to work together need to understand how the pragmatic and judgmental practice of the law differs from the explanatory and relativistic practice of anthropology. By way of introduction, these differences can be viewed in terms of six dimensions.

1. *Locating Liability v. Explanatory Analysis:* The law derives its raison d'être from the need to affix social responsibility. Anthropology does not. Law's purpose is to determine responsibility in human disputes and direct action which will correct, punish, change, ameliorate, or recompense the wrong. Its underlying assumption is that responsibility (even if responsibility is an amoral consequence of social, psychological, environmental, or supernatural forces) can be ascribed to some persons by other persons charged with the duty of doing so. Some moral or normative imperative is

essential to both legal practice and legal thought even for those who believe the sources of the moral imperative can be found in social science data. It does not matter for these purposes whether the moral imperative is ideal or normative; whether it is derived from theology, natural law, logical positivism, or scientific data. The search for the locus of liability in the law guides the scope, content, and quality of truth, information, and explanation in a virtually teleological fashion which distinguishes the legal concept of understanding from the anthropological one.

By contrast, social science, though it studies human thought and behavior, seeks satisfactory explanations outside the responsibility of particular individuals. Its purpose is to provide an explanatory (ideally a predictive) understanding of sociocultural reality.

2. *Judgment v. Relativity.* Law resolves disputes, restores balance, or brings retribution for wrong through changing the behavior of certain parties relative to others. Law rationalizes its mandate to change the obligations and relations of people to one another by judging acts and their consequences. The need to resolve disputes through the modification of human action obliges legal thinkers to use a model which is normative and judgmental (if not necessarily moralistic). This is so regardless of whether one is a devotee of critical legal studies (CLS), a natural law philosopher, or a "liberal" subscribing to neutral principles. Without an acute awareness of the ethical consequences, one cannot be a wise judge, an honest witness, a zealous advocate, or even an earnest party.

In direct contrast, anthropology is best practiced nonjudgmentally. This statement is not naive. No one today would subscribe to the existence, or the advisability, of value-free social science. No one would doubt that norms and values affect the framing of hypotheses; that raw data is refracted in analysis through sociocultural paradigms; or that personality influences participant-observation effects. Yet, just as the practice of law requires an acutely heightened awareness of the moral valence of every movement, the practice of anthropology requires, at a minimum, a temporary suspension of disbelief, and at best a mystical unity with the values, cosmologies, and realities of those most unlike ourselves. Cultural relativity and the celebration of cultural difference remain the core of the anthropological credo. At a minimum, the analysis of data requires some suspension of judgmentality.

3. *The Concrete v. The Wholistic.* Generally, United States courts can only decide matters presenting a concrete "case or controversy." Law is the resolution of specific disputes among real people in real situations. By contrast, anthropological explanation is systemic, wholistic, and abstract. Though it may be derived in part from case studies and specific individuals, it transcends them.

As Rigby and Sevareid (this volume) fully discuss in their chapter, in the practice of law, the abstract principle is applied to the resolution of the specific case, while in anthropology the specific case leads to construction of the abstract model. This is true even where the goal of anthropology is wholly applied—the goal is to change the system; not realign the parties.

4. *Discrete v. Multifactorial Causality.* As fully explained in Davidson's chapter (this volume), in law the meaning of causality is inseparable from the concept of responsibility. The search for legal causality is not a scientific search. It is an inquiry into which person or entity should be held liable for an act, either by having caused it in some controlling or mechanical sense when it was otherwise preventable, or by having failed to stop it, having been in a position to do so.

Completely different is scientific or social scientific causality—an explanation of the multiple happenings or conditions that are responsible for something. Such causality is statistical and probabilistic. Scientific causality neither isolates an individual as having a uniquely causal role nor pinpoints with certainty the fact that "but for" that individual the event would not have taken place. Scientific causality and legal causality are mere homonyms; the latter being synonymous with ascribed responsibility.

5. *Differences in the meaning of fact and truth.* In law, truth ultimately lies in the story told by the human witness of the human act. Despite the growing use of scientific measurement in the courts (e.g., analyzing chemical composition of hair to test for cocaine usage; DNA testing in paternity cases), under state and federal evidence laws measurements do not "speak" for themselves. They can be introduced only if a foundation is laid by a competent witness.

Without the scientific measurements, the human witness alone will suffice. Where help is needed in support of the human witness, that help is spiritual or moral (the certified witnesses of the traditional Islamic courts; the use of a diviner in various customary law systems; swearing on the Bible in a United States court today; or use of "oath helpers" in our court's ancient English ancestors).

The credibility of witnesses is not synonymous with objectivity in a scientific sense. In American common law, the meaning of an "objective" test and a "subjective" test is opposite to the use of those terms in science. Scientifically speaking, "objective" means what is outside the observer; "subjective" what is inside. Legally, when a jury is told to apply a "subjective" test it means to apply the test of what the person on trial thinks—the "outsider" standard. By contrast, when a jury is told to apply an "objective" test, it means the jury should apply the standard that the jury thinks the community or average person subscribes to—an "insider" standard.

Moreover, as Rigby and Sevareid fully discuss, a fact is not an element of raw data, but a finding made by human beings in a moral or normative sociocultural context. This is as true in the American jury system (where fact is found and cases judged by a peer evaluation of the narratives of competing parties) as it is in that quintessentially most informal dispute resolution forum, the Innuit ("Eskimo") song duel (where adversaries sing out the gist of their dispute through ritual insults before the assembled members of their community and the case is judged, that is, fact and truth are found, by a peer evaluation of the narratives of competing parties).

Despite the introspections of interpretive anthropology, the working anthropological assumption, unattainable though it may be, is that the same data, similarly analyzed by equally competent, similarly situated analysts will yield the same results. If not, something is wrong or incomplete. Not so in law. The role of the legal fact finder is decisional. For example, the validity and reliability of the system are not questioned when a retrial after a hung jury leads to a conviction or an acquittal.

6. *Differences in the approach to temporality.* Because the law deals only with concrete situations as they occur, the relationship between the "real" (the specific case or dispute) and the "ideal" (the body of legal and normative precedent) is necessarily intermittent and idiosyncratic. Changed conditions only make changes in legal rules when they are important to decisions in specific cases or are changed by legislation. By contrast human behavior (and to a lesser extent non-institutionalized human norms) evolve continuously. The pursuit of anthropology, especially in the traditional form of extended participant-observation fieldwork, is quite literally the best opportunity to watch microhistory in action as the patterns of social, cultural, and economic relationships within a community change. In fact, it is through such microhistorical studies, bringing the law to account in real time, that legal anthropologists have made some of their most significant recent contributions.

Are these differences inevitable? At least to some extent they are. At bottom, law, even as rarified jurisprudence, is a purposive system for resolution of specific human disputes, with or without restructuring the underlying human relationships; while anthropology, even at its most applied, is a wholistic approach to the analysis of sociocultural systems. The six factors discussed here are perhaps sufficient to cause splitting headaches, not merely double vision. But they are not insurmountable barriers to effective attorney-anthropologist collaborations, provided that anthropologists understand that their expert insights must be comprehensible to, and will inevitably be evaluated within, the rational framework of the law.

Lawyers, Anthropologists, and the Knowledge of Facts

Peter Rigby and Peter Sevareid

Lawyers and anthropologists have different mind sets toward facts. The differences result from their academic training and their beliefs, often unconscious, about the nature of law and human knowledge. Since 1979, the authors and sociologist Robert Kidder have taught an interdisciplinary course in comparative dispute settlement (Lieberman 1988; Sevareid 1986), in which we have observed law students and anthropology students react in strikingly different ways toward the analysis of "facts." For example, in our class we show and discuss Robert Gardner's classic anthropological film *Dead Birds* (Gardner 1963), an account of warfare among the Dani, a Papuan people of the central highlands of New Guinea. The film shows two confederations of Dani men throwing spears at each other. They fight only in the daytime and stop if it begins to rain (so their feathers will not get wet). They fight until one person is killed and then adjourn for a month, one side to celebrate, the other to mourn and cremate the dead.

Gardner has "westernized" his film; editing it to show war and human nature as articulated by the English philosopher Thomas Hobbes. In *Leviathan,* Hobbes (1952[1651]) said people are by nature selfish, individualistic, and engaged in a "war of all against all." In society they form government, a "social contract" with each other, to escape the anarchy of their natures.

Law students accept the scenes of the film as portrayals of "facts." They use the facts as "evidence" in support of an argument for a known accepted principle: the Hobbesian view of society. They do not question whether the film gives a true account of human character in a "state of nature," or an accurate record of Dani life. They say things like: "We need 'law' because human beings are violent"; "The adversary legal system and organized sports are necessary because people are naturally aggressive"; or "This is why dispute settlement without written laws imposed by a strong government won't work."

Anthropology students react differently. Their first reaction is to question the "facts." Does the film accurately portray Dani warfare? Is it indigenous or a product of colonialism? Has the filmmaker imposed Western categories? They question the relationship between Gardner's theories and the film.[1]

These differing responses reflect differences in epistemology (that branch of philosophy concerned with the origins, methods, and limits of knowledge) between anthropologists and lawyers. Whether a viewer thinks the "facts" shown in *Dead Birds* are true depends on that individual's theory of epistemology.

The answer to why lawyers and anthropologists approach the notion of "facts" differently lies, we think, in their differing curricula. Law students, taught to be "pragmatic," have little training in the philosophical problems that surround notions of "fact." They study appellate court decisions almost exclusively, and concentrate on reasoning correctly about "law." Anthropology students study "broad concepts." Because of anthropology's concern with fieldwork, they are consciously aware of the problems of obtaining and using data.

Thinking Like a Lawyer

"The Rule of Law"

The vision of lawyers has been characterized as "narrow, pragmatic, and anti-intellectual. . . . American lawyers, even academic lawyers, rarely think seriously about broad concepts" (Donahue 1980:28). Lawyers see themselves as pragmatists.

Of course, jurisprudential scholars have developed various rigorous philosophies of law. But in most law schools the emphasis is on training practitioners. Jurisprudence, if offered at all, is an advanced elective course—avoided by the majority of students. Instead, most students absorb by "osmosis" the empiricist, natural law beliefs which dominate the profession.

But lawyers do operate from theory, consciously articulated or not. One of the currently prominent schools of jurisprudence is critical legal studies. It strives to illuminate the socioeconomic and contextual realities behind ostensibly neutral judicial decisions. One critical legal studies scholar, David Kairys, writes:

> [Judges' and lawyers'] particular backgrounds, socialization, and experiences—in which law schools and the practice of largely commercial forms of law play an important role—result in a patterning, a consistency, in the ways they categorize, approach, and resolve social and political conflicts. This is the great source of the law's power: it enforces, reflects, constitutes, and legitimizes dominant social and power relations . . . by means of social actors who largely believe in their own neutrality and the myth of legal reasoning. [1982:5]

The twin "myths" of judicial neutrality and legal reasoning referred to by Kairys comprise the general notion of "the rule of law." Although derived from both Roman and English legal philosophy, modern American lawyers identify the origin of the "rule of law" concept with the struggles in 17th-century England between King and Parliament and the common law courts. The English people strove for "a government of laws and not of men" (Massachusetts Constitution, 1978: Pt. I, Art. XXX).

The rule of law implies the necessity for government and also implies that "government requires some form of control other than through individual commands" (Patterson 1953:101). The rule of law, a concept more "sensed" than articulated by American law students, is rooted in the metaphysical belief that law is "natural" (natural law theory) and not the mere "command of the sovereign" (positivist jurisprudence) (Friedmann 1967:258–260). Law exists independently of people or society; like a natural resource to be "found" by those who reason properly.

Judicial neutrality connotes an open mind free of preconceptions. English common law courts held that judges' decisions must be reasonable. Judges whose decisions were not rational acted *ultra vires,* beyond their powers. "Unreasonable" action is beyond the powers given by law to a "just" government and its courts. Judges who approach a case with preconceptions will not act with reason. They will not "find the law" that is appropriate in the case because they will not reason logically from the "material facts" to the controlling principles of law.

Another aspect of judicial neutrality derives from the natural law concept of natural justice which requires lack of bias on the part of the decision maker. A lack of bias encompasses such things as freedom from bribery and nepotism. What the English common law courts labeled as *ultra vires* questions are denominated "substantive due process" questions under the Fifth and Fourteenth Amendments to the United States Constitution. The subdivisions of natural justice are matters of "procedural due process" in American law. Thus, the contemporary idea of judicial neutrality encompasses both freedom from preconceptions (derived from the concept of *ultra vires*) and freedom from personal bias (derived from the concept of natural justice).

Syllogism and Analogy

Legal reasoning, the other myth to which Kairys refers, connotes the logical process which links the appropriate rule of law to the relevant facts of a case. Legal reasoning ("thinking like a lawyer") is syllogistic and analogical. The syllogistic aspect has three parts: a major premise, a minor premise, and a conclusion. Take the following example, adapted from Mark Kelman's discussion of the Realists' concept of "indeterminacy of language" (Kelman 1987:12).

Assume a town council ordinance prohibits "vehicles" in the town park. A previous case held that bicycles are "vehicles" under the ordinance and were prohibited. In the present case, a young paraplegic was arrested when he entered the park in his wheelchair. Charged with bringing a "vehicle" (his wheelchair) into the park, he was found not guilty.

The court reasoned as follows: people are not permitted to bring vehicles into the park (major premise). However, this case is not like the bicycle case because a wheelchair is as essential for a paraplegic as feet are for a healthy person who can walk in the park (minor premise). Therefore, the ordinance does not apply (conclusion). The overall form of the argument is syllogistic.

Within the syllogism there is also reasoning by analogy. Using "compare and contrast" reasoning, the court concludes that a wheelchair is not like a bicycle because it is the only means of locomotion available to a paraplegic. The material facts of the two cases are dissimilar so the court is not bound to follow the bicycle case precedent. According to Lloyd and Freeman,

> [W]hat is . . . involved [in legal reasoning] is not logical deduction in the strict sense but the rational use of *analogy,* whereby a case is compared with like and unlike, so as to determine the "proper" scope of a legal rule. No analogy is compelling in a purely logical sense as leading to a *necessary* conclusion; but as a practical matter human beings do reason by analogy, and find this in many instances a useful way of arriving at normative or practical decisions. [1985:1142; emphasis in original]

The twin myths of judicial neutrality and legal reasoning are constantly reiterated for law students in the language of judicial decisions. Most required reading in the law school curriculum consists of appellate court cases; the "case method" made prominent by Christopher Columbus Langdell at Harvard in 1870 (Stevens 1983:51–72). Although most American law today originates with legislative acts, law students study statutes piecemeal and indirectly through appellate court decisions which interpret them. They do not study trial transcripts to see the evidence introduced in the case nor do they read the pleadings which describe the event triggering the lawsuit. And, of course, they do not observe the actual events.

Texts are appropriately called casebooks; when statutes and other materials are included in them they are called "supplementary" and often bound separately in paperback. Little attention is given to the growing body of empirical legal studies, such as those published in *Law and Society Review.* With carefully defined exceptions, appellate court opinions accept as "true" the factual statements in trial court opinions and review only for "errors of law."[2]

The "facts" from which an appellate court "opines" the law have journeyed along a continuum of change and abstraction from the raw phenomena of experience. At the first stage of the journey, facts are selected on the basis of their relevance to the issues in a case. In our example of the paraplegic in the park, the weather conditions on the day in question and the color of the paraplegic's hair would be phenomenal "facts"—part of the event. But because they are irrelevant to the legal issues, the court would never even be informed about them. By contrast, the wheelchair would be a "fact in evidence." Thus, the evidence before the judge or jury is already highly selective.

In the next stage of the journey, the trier of fact draws from the evidence the "material" or "ultimate" facts—those which are essential or will be used in forming the court's decision. The "ultimate" fact of our example is that the wheelchair of a paraplegic is not a "vehicle" for purposes of the ordinance. This finding is the end product of the work of the trier of fact in the adjudicatory proceeding.

But the finding that the paraplegic's wheelchair is not a "vehicle" is also "law," established by the court. Future courts will cite this case as establishing the "rule of law" that in this town paraplegics' wheelchairs are not prohibited from going to the park. The facts have now been abstracted out of the world of natural phenomena altogether.

Through the case method of instruction, law students primarily study the abstracted end of the continuum. The "facts" that law students are used to are material or ultimate facts and are a world removed from the "data" studied by anthropology students. But law students are not always aware that their "facts" are selected abstractions. Law schools place heavy emphasis on understanding and criticizing the syllogistic and analogical reasoning of judges in appellate case opinions rather than on the process by which raw data become ultimate facts. The typical law school exam consists of "spotting the issues" lurking in a prepared factual summary, accepted as true.

Extensive work with syllogisms leaves law students with the habit of regarding the minor premises they study as "true." Law students are accustomed to thinking of minor premises as statements of true "facts," of the "truth," of actuality—even though the minor premises of appellate court opinions are "ultimate" or "material" facts. The minor premises of case decisions are much closer to the law end of the continuum than to the raw phenomena end.

By treating "ultimate" facts as though they were raw data, law students are trained to ignore (or at least feign obliviousness to) the contextual and normative aspects of decisions.

In classical logic, syllogisms are true in a closed system where there is no question but that the major premise is true and the minor premise is true. For example, a classic Aristotlean syllogism is: All men are mortal; Socrates is a man; therefore, Socrates is mortal. Socrates is mortal because no one doubts that all men are mortal; nor does anyone doubt that Socrates is a man. But law is not a closed system. Neither the major premise nor the minor premise of a typical appellate court judge's opinion are expressions of "truth." Both are the result of normative judgments. This is why David Kairys calls legal reasoning and judicial neutrality "myths." The normative nature of legal truth has been discussed by Julius Cohen:

> The utilization of symbolic construct is common to the disciplines of both scientist and lawyer. . . . But the difference is . . . in the nature of the use to which they are put. The scientist builds his structures on hypothetical, symbolic elements, hoping ultimately to translate them into propositions that correspond to events observable by direct sense experience. The end he seeks is the establishment of reliable *is* or *fact* judgments. The lawyer starts with facts,

> especially as they have bearing on human relationships in society, but the end he seeks is the imposition of *ought* or *normative* judgments concerning them. The symbols that he utilizes, though they relate to facts, are value-charged. Their purpose is evaluative and incitive; they are the means of deciding between competing claims of individuals or groups in society. Unlike the symbols of science, they are not instruments for discovering; rather they are, in the main, instruments for ordering, for creating. Their primary use is . . . one of maintaining or changing human relationships in society. They are in brief, value symbols. [1963:332; emphasis in original]

Thus, though the minor premise of a court decision is normative, law students are in the habit of thinking of the minor premise as true, as a statement of what is, as a statement of "fact." Also, law students think that major premises are true because their jurisprudence is founded on the metaphysical beliefs of natural law.

Getting the Facts "Straight"

Practicing litigators often complain that law students do not get enough "practical" training in how to understand what are the important "facts" in a case presented by a client. They will say something like: "Once you get the facts straight, the law will take care of itself."

Presumably, the law takes care of itself because natural law dictates the correct major premise once the minor premise is established in a case. Students know where to look for the correct major premise because they have studied the extensive rules in each field through appellate opinions. But what is the process of "getting the facts straight" for lawyers?

William Twining has written on the philosophy of evidence most commonly held in Anglo-American law. (Twining 1982, 1984a, 1984b, and 1985). He states:

> [F]act handling is largely a matter of clear thinking and general knowledge, which should have been adequately developed before law school by general education. . . . We are told that the logic appropriate to reasoning about evidentiary issues is the ordinary inductive reasoning used in everyday practical affairs; that judgments about relevance and about probabilities are based on common sense and the common course of experience. [1984a:35]

Lawyers regard themselves as "pragmatists." Like most anthropologists, lawyers approach the notion of "facts" grounded in a 19th-century positivistic empiricism. Twining characterizes the epistemology underlying the law of evidence as "English empiricism" (Twining 1984a:35). He outlines its assumptions:

> (a) Events and states of affairs occur and have an existence independently of human observation; true statements are statements which correspond with facts, i.e., real events and states of affairs in the external world.
>
> (b) Present knowledge about past events is in principle possible; in this context, "knowledge" means warranted beliefs that satisfy specified standards of proof relating to the truth of statements about facts in the real world.

(c) Present knowledge about past events is typically based upon incomplete evidence; it follows from this that establishing the truth about alleged past events is typically a matter of probabilities or likelihoods falling short of complete certainty.

(d) Judgments about the probable truth of allegations about past events must, generally speaking, be based on the available "stock of knowledge" about the common course of events in the external world. In any given society at a particular time, the "stock of knowledge" includes, in a descending scale of probability, generalizations accepted by the scientific community as established, the opinions of experts and "common-sense" generalizations based on the experience of members of society. [1985:13–14]

The first exponent of empiricism, John Locke, believed that ideas are derived from experience; there are no innate ideas or principles (Twining 1985:253–254). Modern lawyers and law students, who approach legal reasoning, albeit unconsciously, from the metaphysical beliefs of natural law, approach facts, also unconsciously, from the method of the empiricists. Thus the mindset of lawyers and law students is a combination of two very different and conflicting philosophical traditions.

Thinking Like an Anthropologist

Being Scientific

Since the beginnings of its professionalization as an academic discipline, the practitioners of anthropology have been concerned to establish it as a "science"; uncritically importing the method of reasoning of the natural sciences. The "scientific method" of the natural sciences makes statements (findings) using inductive logic about the common elements of particular cases that have been observed (experiments). These findings, for the most part, are probabilities, not certainties or "absolute truths."

For example, the conclusion that "women in matrilineal societies have more status than women in patrilineal societies" is arrived at as follows: numerous studies of matrilineal societies show that women in these societies have a high status; specific studies of patrilineal societies show that women have a low status; therefore, it is probable that women in matrilineal societies have a higher status than women in patrilineal societies. In anthropology, "scientific method" is using inductive logic to reason from data to generalized statements.

Traditionally, the dominant epistemological approach of anthropologists is that of 19th-century English empiricists. "Events and states of affairs occur and have an existence independently of human observation; true statements are statements which correspond with facts, i.e., real events and states of affairs in the external world" (Twining 1985:13). A tree falling in the forest makes a sound whether anyone hears it or not. Thus, anthropologists share the epistemological view of lawyers.

However, because anthropologists consider themselves scientists, they "eschew appeal to what is in principle beyond experience" (Manicas

1987:9).[3] Proper anthropologists have no room in their work for metaphysical theories like the natural law beliefs held by law students and lawyers. Validity depends on proof. Historically, a majority of anthropologists have believed that their work is "value free."

But "value free" anthropology is as much of a myth as are judicial neutrality and legal reasoning. Experimental science requires that there be a theory first in the mind of the scientist which is then tested against the data observed. The theory enables the scientist to select which raw data, which "facts," of all the possible data will be tested. The experimental method is by its very nature highly selective as to facts.

Also, the selection of which theory to test involves judgment and "values." By choosing the values in one theory the contrary values in another theory are excluded. For example, a finding that women in matrilineal societies have greater status than women in patrilineal societies may be the conclusion from anthropological fieldwork (experimentation) in both matrilineal and patrilineal societies. But the theory being tested, whether women have a greater status in matrilineal societies than in patrilineal, assumes that in all societies either men or women rank more highly. But this is not always the case. In many egalitarian societies, like the pastoral Ilparakuyo Maasai of Tanzania, to rank order the status of men and women is inappropriate. The Ilparakuyo divide generations into "age sets" with well defined roles for males and females. The roles of the one are not necessarily superior to the roles of the other (see Rigby 1985, 1987–88, and 1992).

If an anthropologist is testing a theory constructed in terms of status, he will selectively analyze data that suggest status. He may find status even if it is not there. It is impossible to look at all the facts of a society in an unbiased, value free manner. Without selecting particular data to study, the anthropologist would be overwhelmed by the totality of information. But the very process of selecting a theory to make the data manageable presupposes a value judgment.

Relating Fact and Theory

Because of the potpourri of historical theories that anthropology students study and the emphasis on fieldwork and research methods in their curriculum, anthropology students have a self-conscious awareness of the relationship between fact and theory which law students, by and large, do not share.

The anthropology curriculum begins with the history of anthropology.[4] Students learn a variety of theories to explain social behavior. Students also learn how anthropology established a credo of fieldwork conducted by appropriate research methods. This credo holds that ethnographic fieldwork should be "done by trained anthropologists who have carefully learned techniques calling for objective and penetrating observation and interviewing, emphatic rapport, and accurate reporting" (Hoebel and Weaver 1979:12–13).

Students also take one or more courses in research method and study the field's major writers, often chronologically, immersing themselves in a dialectical discourse on the relationship between theory and fact.

They often begin by evaluating the epistemology of the 19th-century grand evolutionary theorists William Robertson, Lewis Henry Morgan, Frederick Engels, Sir Henry S. Maine, Sir Edward Burnett Tylor, and Sir James Frazer, in the context of the historical reconstruction instigated by Franz Boas which dominated anthropology from 1900 to 1925.[5] Boas (1858–1942), trained in mathematics and physics, sought "to convert anthropology from the *deductive* speculations of the evolutionists to the *inductive* exactitude of natural science" (Hoebel and Weaver 1979:33) (emphasis added). His *Tsimshian Mythology* (1916) is a work of "empirical anthropology" on the beliefs of the Northwest Coast Indians (Hoebel and Weaver 1979:32). He developed "objective" methods of ethnographic fieldwork. Informants' statements were recorded in their native tongues in a system of phonetic markings he invented. Boas made extensive field observations and developed statistical techniques, methods of controlled comparison, and areal analysis. He stressed that cultural traits should be analyzed in context.

With Boas, anthropology became professionalized as an academic "science." The Boasian reconstruction changed research method and disdained simplistic grand theory. But epistemologically, anthropologists still believed in the objective "real world" of the English empiricists. Turn-of-the-century Boasians grappled with the proper method for clearly seeing the real world; they did not dwell on whether there were inherent limits to its visibility.

The French sociologist Emile Durkheim (1858–1917) strongly influenced anthropology after 1930. Durkheim himself was strongly influenced by Auguste Comte (1798–1857), founder of the positivist school of philosophy. Comte's *The Course of Positive Philosophy* (1830–42) saw intellectual development in three stages: theological (attributing cause to supernatural forces); metaphysical (where metaphysical abstractions were causes); and positive (where phenomena are explained through observation, hypotheses, and experimentation). For positivists, knowledge is founded exclusively on experience and the positive sciences. Positivism has been a mainstay of the exponents of scientific method.

Although Durkheim himself did not do fieldwork and was fascinated with the grand societal design, he stressed empiricism, careful method, and epistemology. If sociology (and thus anthropology) was to be a distinctive scientific discipline, amenable to study and advancement by a group of professionals, Durkheim pondered how its scientific area of knowledge could be privileged and distinct from both other "sciences" (such as biology and psychology), and what he called "common sense" (since social knowledge is common to all members of a particular society).

Durkheim's solution: "The first and most fundamental rule," he stated in *The Rules of Sociological Method,* is *"consider social facts as things"* (Durkheim 1938:14) (emphasis in original). He wrote:

> When I fulfill my obligations as brother, husband, or citizen, when I execute my contracts, I perform duties which are defined, externally to myself and my acts, in law and in custom. Even if they conform to my own sentiments and I feel their reality subjectively, such reality is still objective, for I did not create them; I have inherited them through my education. . . . [Social facts are a category of things that must exist] . . . "outside the individual [subjective] consciousness of the actor" [Durkheim 1938:1–2]

In other words, Durkheim sought to objectify subjective facts. Students learn to question Durkheim's theory because it leaves little room for individual creativity and personal experience.

Functional anthropology was further developed by Bronislaw Malinowski (1884–1942) who, like Boas, had studied mathematics. Malinowski was in Australia when World War I began and was interned. He spent the war in the Trobriand Islands, east of Papua New Guinea, which were then under the colonial authority of the Australian government. His first major work on the Trobriand Islanders, *Argonauts of the Western Pacific* (1961[1922]), established an enduring standard for ethnographic fieldwork. He stressed that an anthropologist must record what people do (however trivial) and what they say. Every aspect of a culture is functionally important in the context of the whole.

Malinowski also developed the notion of "participant-observer," that the best way to understand a culture is to become as much a part of it as possible. "Out of such plunges into the life of the natives . . . I have carried away a distinct feeling that . . . their manner of being became more transparent and easily understandable than it had been before" (Malinowski 1961[1922]:21–22, as quoted by Geertz 1988:77).

Malinowski grappled with the problems of authoritativeness in the presentation of his ethnographic facts; for him there was a "gap" between empirical observation and representation. To Malinowski the utilization of the methodology of "direct observation" in the field was no guarantee of the self-evident validity of anthropological "facts." Authority had to be demonstrated in the presentation of the facts:

> In the field one has to face a chaos of facts, some of which are so small that they seem insignificant; others loom so large that they are hard to encompass with one synthetic glance. But in this crude form they are not scientific facts at all; they are absolutely elusive, and can be fixed only by interpretation, by seeing them *sub specie aeternitatis* [as an eternal subspecies], by grasping what is essential in them and fixing this. *Only laws and generalizations are scientific facts,* and fieldwork consists only and exclusively in the interpreta-

> tion of the chaotic social reality, in subordinating it to general rules. [Malinowski 1954(1948):238, as quoted by Geertz 1988:81; emphasis in original]

> I consider that only such ethnographic sources are of unquestionable scientific value, in which we can clearly draw the line between, on the one hand, the results of direct observation and of native statements and interpretations, and on the other, the inferences of the author. [Malinowski 1961(1922):2–3, as quoted by Geertz 1988:81–82]

Still, Malinowski did not recognize the problematic nature of the "scientific paradigm" that he and his contemporaries applied. The naive epistemology of the natural sciences remained the norm in anthropology.

A. R. Radcliffe-Brown (1888–1955), who published *The Andaman Islanders* (1922) about a people who live on islands in the Bay of Bengal, refocused British social anthropology on social structure (the system of statuses by which individuals relate to each other in socially determined roles). Radcliffe-Brown concentrated on the structure of corporate groups—such as lineages, clans, and age grades—as they engaged in political, religious, and economic activities.

Anthropology students are taught that Radcliffe-Brown was never troubled by epistemological issues. Social relations were, for him, empirically observable in the behavior of individuals in interaction with one another in a community; a "network" of relations easily uncovered by the participant-observation method of fieldwork.

> Let us consider what are the concrete, observable facts with which the social anthropologist is concerned. If we set out to study, for example, the aboriginal inhabitants of a part of Australia, we find a certain number of individual human beings in a certain natural environment. We can observe the acts of behavior of these individuals, including, of course, their acts of speech, and the material products of past actions. We do not observe a "culture," since that word denotes, not any concrete reality, but an abstraction, and as it is commonly used a vague abstraction. But direct observation does reveal to us that these human beings are connected by a complex network of social relations. I use the term "social structure" to denote this network of *actually existing social relations*. It is this that I regard as my business to study if I am working, not as an ethnologist or psychologist, but as a social anthropologist. I do not mean that the study of social structure is the whole of social anthropology, but I do regard it as the most fundamental part of the science. [Radcliffe-Brown 1952:189–190; emphasis added]

Students thus see that Radcliffe-Brown, like Malinowski, operated from the naive epistemology of the natural sciences.

Another epistemological shift in the history of anthropology occurred after the Second World War with the publication of the writings of the French anthropologist Claude Lévi-Strauss, founder of "social structuralism," who revitalized the Durkheimian tradition. Previous functionalists and structuralists had been "more interested in the differences between human cultures than in their overall similarity" (Leach 1974:7). And their method of work had been to spend long years in the field, first learning the language and then making detailed records of a single society. This was often followed by a lifetime of analyzing and writing up the results of their research. "Their aims and methods . . . [were] those of natural science— a movement *from* specific, empirical research *toward* general classification of types of societies and the formulation of cultural laws of social organization" (Hoebel and Weaver 1979:37; emphasis in original). Harking back to the period of anthropological writing before Franz Boas, Lévi-Strauss was interested in discovering general principles that apply to the structures of all societies rather than finding principles that define the differences between societies. He was particularly concerned with the structures of primitive thought which he felt were present in modern minds.

Anthropology students learn that Lévi-Strauss was important for the notion of "facts" because he signaled a shift in epistemological belief. His "structuralism" was grounded in a dialectical theory of knowledge that differed radically from the empiricism of anthropologists like Boas, Malinowski, and Radcliffe-Brown, for whom the hard natural sciences, like physics and Darwinian evolutionary biology, had been the models. From Lévi-Strauss to the present, other outside disciplines have driven the changes in anthropological theory. For Lévi-Strauss the major influences were structural linguistics and Karl Marx's concept of the production of knowledge.

The line of thinking that culminated in French social structuralism began with the Italian philosopher and jurist Giambattista Vico (1668–1744) whose book *The New Science* (1948[1725]) proposed a science of human society. To Vico primitive man possesses an innate "poetic wisdom" *(sapienza poetica)* by which he responds to life around him and which he expresses in metaphysically rooted metaphors, symbols, and myths. This poetic myth making creates both human institutions and societies and in turn molds the men and women who live in them. "[M]an constructs the myths, the social institutions, virtually the whole world as he perceives it, and in so doing he constructs himself. This . . . involves the continual creation of recognizable and repeated forms" (Hawkes 1977:14). These forms are *structures.*

Two American linguists who influenced Lévi-Strauss, Edward Sapir (1884–1942) and B. L. Whorf, are known for a "hypothesis" in the Vico tradition that the nature of the culture of a community, and its idea of "facts" and "reality," is structured by the particular language that that community speaks.

> Human beings do not live in the objective world alone . . . but are very much at the mercy of the particular language which has become the medium of expression for their society. It is quite an illusion to imagine that one adjusts to reality essentially without the use of language and that language is merely an incidental means of solving specific problems of communication or reflection. The fact of the matter is that the "real world" is to a large extent built up

> on the language habits of the group. No two languages are ever sufficiently similar to be considered as representing the same social reality. The worlds in which different societies live are distinct worlds, not merely the same world with different labels attached. . . . We see and hear and otherwise experience very largely as we do because the language habits of our community predispose certain choices of interpretation. [Sapir 1949:162, as quoted by Hawkes 1977:31]

Lévi-Strauss was also influenced by Karl Marx's (1818–83) "materialist conception of history," which holds that understanding the organization of productive work (human labor, the means by which subsistence is obtained from nature) is crucial to understanding human history. As Marx said in *Das Kapital:*

> Labor is a process in which both man and nature participate, and in which man of his own accord starts, regulates, and controls the material reactions between himself and nature. . . . By thus acting on the external world and changing it, he at the same time changes his own nature. [Quoted by McLellan 1976:36]

Marx was not an empiricist. He did not believe that anyone could view the world in a totally objective, value-free manner.

Drawing on the tradition of Vico, the American structural linguists, Durkheim, and Marx, Lévi-Strauss argued that when anthropologists study a culture they should not isolate such different elements as kinship, food, marriage laws, and myths. Though these elements may be partially created by deep structures that are the same in all human minds, they are also formed by structures of thought that are influenced by the language of a particular culture. The various elements are partial expressions of a whole culture. Lévi-Strauss used concepts about language to change the way anthropology should go about its work. And he used Marx's notion of the production of knowledge to justify this change. Previous empirical anthropologists had believed that, for example, by isolating facts about kinship in many societies, laws of kinship applicable to all people could be found by reasoning inductively from this data. But facts of kinship do not exist by themselves in the real world. They are created by the culture of each society and cannot be understood without reference to the structures of that culture.

Anthropology students are taught when reading Lévi-Strauss and when learning about the changes in theory that occurred after the Second World War, that the real world of the empiricists is not necessarily denied. The assumption of the postwar anthropological theorists is *not* that reality itself is relative. They don't know whether it is or not. They are uncertain. They question if it is possible to find universal laws about social behavior that will have the validity of specific natural science laws, such as the law of gravity. They ask whether natural science research methods make sense for anthropology. They turn their attention to epistemological concerns, to asking not only how individual cultures create their own knowledge, but also about how anthropologists themselves create anthropological knowledge.

Representing this new anthropological epistemology is Clifford Geertz, a leading "interpretivist." Interested in "the literary character of anthropology" (Geertz 1988:3), Geertz is specifically concerned with "the understanding of understanding" (Geertz 1983:5), as used in recent literary criticism. For him, as for other interpretive anthropologists, the text of what anthropologists have written is the important reality, the facts of interest (Marcus and Fischer 1986:25–26). Geertz is primarily engaged in applying hermeneutics, the theory and methodology of interpretation, to the books written by anthropologists.

Interpretive anthropologists such as Geertz, and practitioners of what has been labeled modern "critical anthropology," espouse a conscious retreat from any attempt to devise encompassing social theory that can deal with all the dimensions of social life. From the evolutionists to the French social structuralists, anthropology sought to establish theories, as generally applicable as possible, about the life of the communities they studied. But with the new anthropology, social theory building is not a primary objective:

> Ours is once again a period rich in experimentation and conceptual risk-taking. Older dominant frameworks are not so much denied—there being nothing so grand to replace them—as suspended. The ideas they embody remain intellectual resources to be used in novel and eclectic ways. [Marcus and Fischer 1986:10]

The danger with interpretive anthropology is that the objects of its discourse can cease to be real peoples engaged in the production and reproduction of their social life and communities. Their achievements and sufferings are merely subjects for "interpretation." Anthropology for some has come to be an enterprise much like the law student's minimalist task of interpreting appellate decisions.

This survey of what anthropology students study shows that their curriculum is composed substantially of the work of anthropologists who held the English empiricists' view of the nature of reality. Though students study other viewpoints—particularly Marx, the French structuralists, and the "critical anthropologists"—our own experience suggests that what sticks in their minds is the empiricists' notion of the nature of facts. This is reinforced by the great deal of time devoted to learning detailed fieldwork techniques. Students have been instilled with the desire to question the accuracy of particular facts, not with doubt that the "true" facts may never be known because "reality" may depend on the viewpoint of the anthropologist gathering the facts. Most graduate with the belief that they are "scientists" and as scientists their life work should be the discovery of the underlying natural laws of society.

Conclusion

Law students and anthropology students react differently to the film *Dead Birds* because the curricula they study are different. Law students have had comparatively little training in the handling of facts. Because they concentrate on appellate court opinions, they accept as absolutely true "facts" which in reality are highly selected by judges to substantiate the rules of law those judges wish to apply.

Anthropology students are critical of the presentation of facts because of their study of the writings of anthropologists whose theoretical frameworks vary and the emphasis in their curriculum on fieldwork and research methods. These students study theory first; they then select a theory which they test by empirical research. They have been taught that this "scientific" method leads to the establishment of propositions which are only *probably* "true."

To put these differences in Aristotelian terms, law students use a method of reasoning which is "apodictic" (Berman 1977:900–912). Expressing themselves in deductive syllogisms, they reason from major premises which they consider to be indisputable. (Law students are encouraged to treat the premise "people are not permitted to bring vehicles into the park" as if it were on the same level of truth as "all men are mortal.") But legal truths are normative, not indisputable. And they remain normative—remain value judgments—even when they are presented using an apodictic method.

At the same time, law students (and lawyers) maintain a 19th-century English empiricist's faith in the reality of facts. That is, there is an external world independent of human beings (a tree falling in the forest makes a sound whether anyone hears it or not). And, for law students, court cases express indisputable truths about these facts as a result of judicial apodictic reasoning expressed by way of syllogism. The independently existing set of facts that a wheelchair is not a vehicle (minor premise), when syllogistically coupled with the applicable rule of law that only vehicles are prohibited in the park (major premise), leads to the indisputable result (conclusion) that a wheelchair is not prohibited from entering the park.

On the other hand, anthropology students (and anthropologists) reason, in Aristotle's terms, not apodictically but dialectically. In dialectical reasoning premises are usually disputable; they are not certainties but only probabilities (for example, women in matrilineal societies have more status than women in patrilineal societies). Dialectical reasoning prefers to express itself in inductive logic rather than in syllogistic logic. Inductive logic reasons from experience to probability by finding the common facts in the individual cases that have been observed. (For example, numerous studies of matrilineal societies show that women in these societies have a high status; therefore, it is probable that women in matrilineal societies have a higher status than women in patrilineal societies.) The dialectical method when expressed in inductive logic is the "scientific" method of anthropologists.

Lawyers and anthropologists both believe in an external world of reality. But lawyers believe that they can objectively look at facts in the real world without preconceptions; that if they "get the facts straight" the "law will take care of itself." Judges believe that it is possible for them to be objective and neutral. Although the opposing parties in a case may distort the facts by presenting only those facts which support their respective positions, an unbiased judge can see the "true" facts.

The problem with this, of course, is that judicial neutrality and legal reasoning are myths. They are myths because judges are not looking at the facts of a case without preconceptions. It is impossible to select the relevant facts of a case from all the possible facts that surround an event in the real world without having a theory first, a "theory of the case." The minor premise of a law case syllogism is not just a listing of raw facts; it is a highly selective, characterized version of the facts. To say that "a wheelchair is not a vehicle" is to make a judgment that is more toward the law end of the continuum than the fact end. Judges have a theory in mind, consciously or unconsciously, when they look at the raw facts. They reason from this theory about the raw facts to reach the minor premise of a case. Once they have the minor premise, there can be but one relevant major premise to couple with it. And once a judge has characterized a wheelchair as not being a vehicle, there can be but one apodictic conclusion. In other words, judges think they are arriving at *is* or *fact* conclusions when what they have made are normative judgments. Our law students made the assumption that the Dani in *Dead Birds* were engaging in Hobbesian warfare because they viewed the facts of Dani warfare from a theoretical perspective, from a theory of the case, that knows only one kind of warfare: the kind of warfare that Hobbesian human beings fight. Human beings are Hobbesian for lawyers because that is part of their unconscious natural law belief system.

When dealing with lawyers, anthropologists should be aware that lawyers believe, perhaps unconsciously, in natural law. Although many anthropologists have become "impatient" with metaphysical beliefs (Hoebel and Weaver 1979:32), they must curb this impatience or they will miss much of what is going on. At the same time, however, anthropologists should also be aware that they themselves deal in conclusions that are only probable, not absolute. Their own reasoning process is dialectic and not apodictic. For successful collaborations both attorneys and anthropologists must remember that they bring different mind-sets to the problems at hand.

Notes

[1]The questions asked by anthropology students actually parallel an intense anthropological debate surrounding the editing and purpose of *Dead Birds* which followed its release. For fuller discussion see Heider's (1979) *Grand Valley Dani: Peaceful Warriors*.

[2]The Anglo-American common law notion that "fact" and "law" are separate things came from the historical need to differentiate between that part of the judicial process that was within the power of the jury and that part which was within the power of the judge. Today, when an appellate court considers questions of fact, it does so only when it is looking for such egregious errors by the trial court that the appellate court can say the findings of facts are unreasonable or *ultra vires* and thus wrong as a "matter of law" or when expressly authorized to undertake *de novo* review under particular statutes.

[3]Interestingly, the first systematic anthropology was done by two Catholic missionaries, who wrote from the confidence of a metaphysical belief system: the Spanish Franciscan, Fray Bernardino de Sahagun, who worked in Mexico in the 16th century, and the French Jesuit Father Joseph Francois Lafitau whose book, *Customs of the American Savages, Compared with Customs of Early Times,* published in Paris in 1724, contrasted the Hurons and Iroquois with early Greece and Rome.

[4]Widely used beginning college texts such as Hoebel and Weaver's *Anthropology and the Human Experience* give an overview of the undergraduate and graduate curricula in anthropology. We find it significant that there is no similar single-volume introductory overview commonly read by law students.

[5]Among the great works of the 19th-century evolutionary theorists are Lewis Henry Morgan's *Systems of Consanguinity and Affinity of the Human Family* (1870) (a study of kinship and social structure) and *Ancient Society, or Researches in the Lines of Human Progress from Savagery through Barbarism to Civilization* (1877); Friedrich Engles's *The Origin of the Family, Private Property, and the State in the Light of the Researches of Lewis H. Morgan* (1970[1884]) (which used Marx's notes on Morgan to link private property, the monogamous patriarchal family, and the state to the degradation of women and the exploitation of workers); Sir Henry Maine's *Ancient Law* (1905) (concluding "that the movement of the progressive societies has hitherto been a movement *from Status to Contract*" [1905:41; emphasis in original]; Sir Edward Burnett Tylor's *Primitive Culture* (1871) (establishing the anthropological concept of culture) and Sir James Frazer's monumental study of magic and religion, *The Golden Bough* (1890).

Law, Science, Causality, and Proof

Michael Davidson

When anthropologists testify as expert witnesses, they often wonder whether what they know is what the "law" wants to find out. They worry about how the law will interpret and use what they say. As an anthropologist turned attorney, I am well aware of the cognitive clash between legal and scientific paradigms. Anthropological experts can gain substantial understanding of how the judicial process uses expert testimony from the extensively developed law regarding the testimony of experts from the various biological sciences. My own area of expertise—products liability (or toxic tort) law, the right to sue for damages for disease and injury resulting from harmful products—is a good example.

In American legal ideology, a manufacturer may be held responsible for damages when an individual who has had contact with the manufacturer's product develops a chronic illness if it can be legally proved that the product "caused" the illness. Scientists are asked to provide testimony about "cause." But expert witnesses soon realize that although lawyers and scientists use the same words they do not speak the same language: "cause," "proof," and "evidence" mean very different things in different disciplinary cultures.

In tort litigation, scientific testimony is assessed according to legal standards of "truth," which are inseparable from the legal purpose of allocating responsibility. Theoretically, tort law deters harmful behavior by allocating the costs of injuries directly to those who cause them. Historically, the concept of "negligence" is the core of tort law. For example, if, while racing 70 miles per hour through a blizzard, an automobile driver hits someone, the driver may be held liable for failure to behave like a "reasonably prudent person." Essentially, negligence is a legally significant form of carelessness which makes someone blameworthy so that the assessment of damages seems fair. But the social adjudication of responsibility is as important as "factual" cause. Therefore, the law sometimes imposes a special burden on a party who acted dangerously or who can best distribute the costs of the injury. For example, in the famous case of *Sommers v. Tice,*[1] two hunters negligently fired bird shot. A man was hit. The court shifted the usual burden of proof in tort cases, which requires the injured plaintiff to prove who caused the injury. The court held both shooters responsible, unless one could prove that the other had fired the wounding shot. Products liability law modifies traditional negligence theory even more. It places an affirmative burden on manufacturers to provide safe products. They can be held liable even if they are not careless because they are deemed better able to distribute the costs of injuries than the persons disabled by the products.

Manufacturers are liable for injuries their products cause in three situations: (1) Where there has been a "manufacturing defect" (such as a piece of glass in a jar of food). Liability exists even if no one is negligent and the company's safeguards are unimpeachable. (2) Where there has been a "design defect" which causes injury (such as a car designed with a dangerously located gas tank). A safer design must be available. (3) Where there has been a "failure to warn" (as, for example, failure to advise consumers of a drug's known side effects). In *Beshada v. Johns-Manville,*[2] the court held that the only issue was whether the product (asbestos) was unreasonably safe without a warning. It would not let Johns-Manville testify that the carcinogenic hazards of low level asbestos exposure were scientifically unknown at the time of the injuries. It justified the decision as an incentive to manufacturers to do more research.[3]

Similarly, in claims of prenatal injury to daughters of women who took DES (diethylstilbestrol, a purported miscarriage preventative) during pregnancy, the courts extended the rule of *Sommers v. Tice.* Plaintiffs were generally unable to prove which brand of DES their mothers had taken. The California Supreme Court in *Sindell v. Abbot Laboratories,*[4] held that each manufacturer would be liable in proportion to its share of the DES market, unless it could prove its product had not been taken by plaintiffs' mothers. New York's highest court went even further. In *Hymowitz v. Eli Lilly,*[5] it held all DES manufacturers liable in proportion to market share even if they could prove their product had not been used.

In tort law, then, determining "cause" means deciding who must bear the responsibility for safety and the cost of hazard. Ben Small has described the lawyer's approach to causation: "[H]is is a function of identifying influences towards legal responsibility for harm which may lie in habits and behaviors of the surrounding society in which man and his pathological risks are cast" (Small 1985:651).

Two tort law doctrines reveal how the law uses "cause" as its test to select the "responsible" party from among the factual causes. Liability requires "but-for" causation: "The defendant's conduct is a cause of the event, if the event would not have occurred without it" (Keeton 1984:266). But the defendant's conduct must also be a "proximate cause" near enough in foreseeability and social and economic distance for the imposition of liability to serve a deterrent effect.[6]

While the need to make binding, responsible societal judgments tinges legal truth with an exaggerated moral certainty, the pursuit of scientific truth makes scientists uniquely skeptical of all so-called facts and explanations. There are two principal scientific "truths." The first is that there are no "truths," only hypotheses that have not been disproven. The second is that empirical knowledge is only as good as the study which produced it. When experiments yield results that are consistent with a theory, they may increase subjective faith in the correctness of the theory but they can never prove that the theory is true. Neither can they provide a basis for estimating the probability that the theory is true. The universe of evidence against which to compare the corroborative data is always unknown. Scientific skepticism about empirical facts extends to the methodologies from which facts are derived.[7]

The legal system seeks answers from scientists that science cannot provide: it assesses the truth of expert testimony in legal terms for legal purposes. Experts, unlike eye witnesses, may testify about their opinions and base their opinions on information which would itself be inadmissable as evidence. Federal Rule of Evidence 703 (which has a counterpart in the rules of many states) provides:

> The facts or data in the particular case upon which an expert bases an opinion or inference may be those perceived by or made known to the expert at or before the hearing. If of a type reasonably relied upon by experts in the field in forming inferences or opinions upon the subject, the facts or data need not be admissible in evidence.

The judge or jury relies on the individual opinion of the expert because of his professional qualifications. The judge and jury do not see the data on which the expert forms an opinion. It is not evidence, need not even be admissible in evidence, and is often beyond the lay person's comprehension. The expert is obliged to rely on data normally used by members of her discipline and to reach conclusions in the usual professionally acceptable way.

The disciplines whose perspectives are most compatible with the courts search for causality are not necessarily the most scientifically rigorous ones. For example, even without controlled experimental support for their conclusions, deference is given to the testimony of treating physicians, perhaps because of the social reliance placed on them as diagnosticians and healers. Although scientists have doubted whether cancers can be caused by trauma, the treating physician may be satisfied that in *this* case the cancer was caused by trauma. In *Peterson v. Kansas City Public Service Co.,*[8] and *Menarde v. Philadelphia Transportation Co.,*[9] damages were awarded to women who developed breast cancers on the site of traumatic injuries based on treating physicians' testimony on cause.

A physician's testimony is admissible if she or he can state to a "reasonable degree of medical certainty" that the injury caused the disease. In *Bertram v. Wunning,*[10] a physician had testified that there was a "90% chance" that a plaintiff's hernia was caused by an accident. The court ruled that this did not meet the requisite certainty standard. On retrial, the physician testified that a 90% chance is a "reasonable degree of medical certainty." The court found this sufficient.[11] There is a natural congruence between the lawyer's need to prove "cause" and the treating physician's testimony because both focus on the specific case before them.

By contrast, epidemiological testimony is problematic when there is evidence of a statistical association between exposure to the product and a disease but the disease also occurs without exposure. One court resolved the problem by extending the *Sommers v. Tice* approach and shifting the burden of proof: defendants were required to prove that exposure *had not* caused the disease. The case, *Allan v. United States,*[12] concerned diseases allegedly caused by the downwind effects of nuclear testing. The court reasoned:

> Where a defendant who negligently creates a radiological hazard which puts an identifiable population group at an increased risk, and a member of that group develops a biological condition which is consistent with having been caused by the hazard to which he has been negligently subjected, such consistency having been demonstrated by substantial, appropriate, persuasive, and connecting factors, the fact finder *may* reasonably conclude that the hazard caused the condition absent persuasive proof to the contrary offered by the defendant. [588 F. Supp. 247]

The plaintiff was not required to demonstrate "causation-in-fact" because social policy considerations mandate assigning responsibility to the defendant.

Physicians, pharmacologists, toxicologists, and epidemiologists rely on different data to determine causality. When experts from different disciplines testify on different sides of a case, courts must grapple with rules for deciding the "battle of the experts." Normally courts do not rank order the disciplines by rigor of proof. Rather, they allow all qualified experts to testify and direct the "trier of fact" (often the jury, sometimes the judge) to decide.

For example, in *Ferebee v. Chevron Chemical Co.,*[13] a jury awarded damages based upon the claim that an agricultural research worker had contracted pulmonary fibrosis from dermal exposure to paraquat. The treating physician testified that, based on the clinical history and his knowledge of three similar cases, he believed paraquat had caused the fibrosis. Epidemiologists and toxicologists testified for the defense that, by the standards accepted in their disciplines, the available evidence did not support a conclusion that dermal exposure to paraquat was a cause of pulmonary fibrosis.

The appellate court affirmed, describing the case as a "classic battle of the experts, a battle in which the jury must decide the winner" (*Id.* at 1535). It explained:

> A cause-effect relationship need not be clearly established by animal or epidemiological studies before a doctor can testify that, in his opinion, such a relationship exists. As long as the basic methodology employed to reach such a conclusion is sound, such as use of tissue samples, standard tests, and patient examination, product liability law does not preclude recovery until a "statistically significant" number of people have been injured or until science has had the time and resources to complete sophisticated laboratory

> studies of the chemical. In a courtroom, the test for allowing a plaintiff to recover in a tort suit of this type is not scientific certainty but legal sufficiency; if reasonable jurors could conclude from the expert testimony that paraquat more likely than not caused Ferebee's injury, the fact that another jury might reach the opposite conclusion or that science would require more evidence before conclusively considering the causation question resolved is irrelevant. That Ferebee's case may have been the first of its exact type, or that his doctors may have been the first alert enough to recognize such a case, does not mean that the testimony of those doctors, who are concededly well qualified in their fields, should not have been admitted. [*Id.* at 1535]

The court, in effect, concluded that testimony was legally sufficient if it met the professional standards of the testifying scientist's discipline. As long as there was evidence based on *some* science it was a question of "fact" for the jury which science they would rely on.

The rules of evidence require that the facts or data on which an expert forms an opinion be of a type usual in the expert's field but there is no requirement that the conclusions themselves be shared by other members of the discipline. *Wells v. Ortho Pharmaceutical Corp.,*[14] is a case in point. The issue was whether a spermicide had caused an infant's birth defects. The trial judge found that the scientific studies themselves were inconclusive on the issue of causation, but he held that legally the spermicide had caused some of the infant's birth defects. The judge had found the pharmacologist who testified for the plaintiff more credible than the epidemiologist who testified for the defense. The appellate court sustained a multimillion dollar verdict, provoking the ire of the scientific community. A *New York Times* editorial of December 27, 1986, declared that a Federal Food and Drug Administration (FDA) panel had found the preponderance of the evidence indicated no association between the spermicide and birth defects; that "the Federal judiciary has placed itself opposite the best judgment of the scientific community"; and that the *New England Journal of Medicine* had complained that the medical community was concerned that "the courts will not be bound by reasonable standards of proof."

The researchers who had first reported the association were sufficiently chagrined by the *Wells* case to publish letters commenting on the case in the *Journal of the American Medical Association* (1986). Of the five authors, one reexamined the data, finding error due to a misclassification of the exposed population; three stated that caveats in the article cautioned against causal interpretations. The fifth stated that the "article should never have been published." He wrote:

> In our present litigious environment, the reservations and qualifications written into a published report are often ignored, and the article is used as "proof" of a causal relationship. It would have been much more appropriate for our findings to have gone through the more traditional process of being discussed among colleagues at scientific meetings. In this process, the issues we raised and others would have been discussed among investigators. This winnowing process could have altered the way the manuscript was written or

might have delayed its submission until more information was available. [Holmes 1986:3096]

Judicial uncertainty over whether to judge an expert's conclusions against the consensus of the scientific community is exemplified by two cases which, on the basis of virtually identical testimony, have come down on opposite sides on the issue of whether the antinausea drug Bendectin causes birth defects. In *Richardson v. Richardson-Merrell, Inc.,*[15] the court set aside a $1.6 million verdict for the plaintiff, reasoning that no reasonable jury could have found it more likely than not that the plaintiff's birth defects had been caused by exposure to Bendectin because the epidemiological evidence showed no association and the toxicological evidence was insufficient by accepted toxicological standards. In rejecting the testimony of plaintiff's expert, Dr. Dune, the court reasoned:

> Though Dr. Dune might disagree, there is a universally held scientific consensus that Bendectin has not been shown to be a teratogen, and the issue being a scientific one, reasonable jurors could not reject that consensus without indulging in precisely the same speculation and conjecture which the multiple investigations undertook, but failed, to confirm. That Dr. Dune remains an unbeliever and was willing to testify to his disbelief "with reasonable medical certainty" does not mandate that this case be left as the jury decided it. [*Id.* at 799]

The appellate court affirmed.

In another Bendectin case employing almost the same evidence, the trial judge also reversed a jury verdict for the plaintiff. But in *Oxendine v. Merrell Dow,*[16] a different appellate court reinstated the jury verdict on *Ferebee* grounds, holding that in a "battle of the experts" the judge should not second guess the jury.

Ultimately, a toxic tort case is tried to a jury because the scientific evidence of causation is merely one factor in the determination of what is, essentially a judgment about social responsibility.

Notes

[1]Sommers v. Tice, 33 Cal. 2d 80, 199 P.2d (Sup. Ct. Cal. 1948).

[2]Beshada v. Johns-Manville, 90 N.J. 191, 447 A.2d 539 (Sup. Ct. of N.J. 1982).

[3]But the New Jersey Supreme Court would not extend the rule to a pharmaceutical case. Fedlman v. Ledlerle Laboratories, 97 N.Y. 429, 479 A.2d 374 (Sup. Ct. of N.J. 1984).

[4]Sindell v. Abbot Laboratories, 26 Cal. 3d 588, 607 P.2d 924 (Sup. Ct. of Cal.), *cert. denied,* 449 U.S. 912 (1980).

[5]Hymowitz v. Eli Lilly, 73 N.Y.2d 487, 539 N.E.2d 1069, 541 N.Y. Supp. 2d 941 (1989).

[6]Palsgraf v. The Long Island Railroad, 248 N.Y. 339, 162 N.E. 99 (Ct. of Appeals 1928), is the classic proximate cause case. A man carrying a package jumped unsteadily aboard a moving train. Two station guards tried to steady him, making the package fall. It contained fireworks which exploded, dislodging a platform scale which hurt Mrs. Palsgraf. Accepting that the guards negligence met the "but for" cause requirement, the court found the injury was not reasonably foreseeable. Hence, there was no proximate cause and the railroad was not liable.

[7]Scientists have actively debated the productive value of short-term tests to determine human carcinogens. One study found that 35 percent of the substances classified as human

carcinogens were negative in short-term tests. Another found that 60 percent of chemicals believed to be noncarcinogenic in rodent assays, produced positive results in short-term tests (Johnson and Snell 1986).

They have similarly debated the value of long-term bioassays. Since species differ in toxic tolerance, metabolism, pharmacokinetics, and other factors, what is carcinogenic to one species may be harmless to another.

Scientists recognize that results can differ significantly between laboratories. One study found poor agreement between two laboratories in production of lung adenomas in Strain A mice using the same set of chemicals (Maronpot et al. 1986).

Different methods can also produce different results. In a recent study researchers tested the same hypothesis in a hospital population by two methods: the observational study found an association between infant formula supplementation and reduced breast-feeding rates; the controlled clinical trial found no association. They attributed the difference, in part, to self-selection in the observational study (Gray-Donald and Kramer 1988). An article by Alvan Feinstein (1988) lists 546 different relationships in which the results of one epidemiologic study were contradicted by another.

[8]Peterson v. Kansas City Public Service Co., 259 S.W. 789 (Sup. Ct. of Missouri 1953).

[9]Menarde v. Philadelphia Transportation Co., 376 Pa. 497, 103 A.2d 681 (Sup. Ct. of Pa. 1953).

[10]Bertram v. Wunning, 417 S.W.2d 120 (St. Louis Ct. of Appeals 1967).

[11]For a recent review and discussion of standards of statistical evidence as evidence in tort cases see Cranor and Nutting 1990.

[12]Allan v. United States, 588 F. Supp. 247, (C.D. Utah 1984).

[13]Ferebee v. Chevron Chemical Co., 736 F.2d 1529 (D.C. Cir. 1984).

[14]Wells v. Ortho Pharmaceutical Corp., 88 F.2d 741 (11th Cir. 1986), *cert. denied,* 479 U.S. 361 (1987).

[15]Richardson v. Richardson-Merrell, Inc., 649 F. Supp. 799 (D.D.C. 1986), *aff'd,* 857 F.2d 823 (D.C. Cir. 1988).

[16]Oxendine v. Merrell Dow, 506 F.2d 1100 (D.C. Cir. 1986). Also, courts may find that much more rigorous evidence of causation is needed to prove a case than to settle it or to promulgate safety regulations. In the *Agent Orange* cases, a class consisting of Vietnam War veterans claimed illnesses resulting from exposure to dioxin. Judge Weinstein approved a $180 million settlement although he concluded that the available epidemiological data did not support the claim. But some plaintiffs had "opted out" of the class settlement, hoping for greater damages at trial. The judge found their evidence inadmissible because the epidemiological data showed no greater incidence of the diseases in the exposed population than the general population and the animal studies involving different species were of so little probative force and so potentially misleading as to be inadmissible and unacceptable as a predicate for expert testimony under Federal Rule of Evidence 703. *In re* Agent Orange Product Liability Litigation, 611 F. Supp. 1223, 1239, 1241 (E.D.N.Y. 1985), Judge Weinstein described the difference between proof sufficient for regulation and that necessary for compensation:

> [T]he distinction between avoidance of risk through regulation and compensation for injuries after the fact is a fundamental one. In the former, regulation may lead to control of a toxic substance even though the probability of harm to any individual is small and the studies necessary to assess the risk are incomplete, society as a whole is willing to pay the price as a matter of policy. In the latter, a far higher probability (greater than 50%) is required since the law believes it unfair to require an individual to pay for another's tragedy unless it is shown that it is more likely than not that he caused it. [*In re* Agent Orange Product Liability Litigation, at 781, (E.D.N.Y. 1985)]

II. Two Case Studies of Effective Anthropological Experts

Anthropology and Capital Case Litigation

Isabel Wright

I watched the 12 jurors for the penalty phase of this California murder trial file back into the courtroom. After deliberating for eight days, they had reached a unanimous decision on whether the defendant would receive the death penalty or be granted life in prison without parole. They sank wearily into the seats they had gotten to know so well during the ten-week trial, studiously avoiding the eyes of the other major protagonists. Despite the past two days of flying rumors, only they knew what the verdict would be.

The defendant, a young African-American man, hunched over the faded brown folder holding his legal papers and anxiously scanned each juror's face. From the corner of his eye, he caught sight of his attorney—a middle-aged white man with 15 years of experience in the Public Defender's office. Feigning confidence, the attorney appeared relaxed. The defendant sat back finally and stared at the judge. Whatever the jurors had decided now, he knew that their earlier verdict that he was guilty of murder with special circumstances meant he would die in prison. But he also knew that if even one person on the jury had been moved by the story of his life, told through witnesses and argument at this separate, constitutionally required, penalty phase trial, he would be spared death in the gas chambers.

My role in this case had begun as an expert witness. Under the mandates of the United States Supreme Court opinions in *Furman v. Georgia*[1] and *Gregg v. Georgia*[2] and the California death penalty law (the "Briggs Statute"), a trial where a defendant faces a possible death sentence must consist of two parts. In the first part, the jury judges guilt or innocence of the crime. In the second, so-called penalty phase, the jury determines whether a guilty defendant should live or die. In reaching its verdict, the jury considers whether evidence presented about the personality and background of the defendant aggravates the crime, compelling death, or mitigates it, requiring life.

As an anthropologist, I testify for the defense about how a defendant's social, cultural, and economic background and life history impact on his or her commission of a crime. It is my job to make the defendant's behavior humanly comprehensible to the jury by explaining the context that produced it. I work as part of the defense team and use my objective skills and insights to help the defendant's case. As an expert, I review and analyze interviews by defense investigators and examine public records. I attempt to validate this data by interviewing the defendant and key witnesses, and by conducting further research into the records before coming to my opinion. Usually I research and construct a full social history. Sometimes I testify in court. More often, I consult "behind the scenes" with the attorney on how the social history should be presented through lay and expert testimony and on which mitigating factors should be stressed as most dominant in the defendant's life.

My Initiation into Death Penalty Work

My involvement in capital cases began serendipitously. During my final year of doctoral study at the University of California at Davis, my husband accepted a promotion requiring us to move from the San Francisco Bay area to southern California. New doctorate in hand, I struggled to find a niche as a practicing anthropologist in greater Los Angeles.

To bolster my sagging spirits and make contacts, I attended a meeting of the Commission for Women. A sociologist named Margo was among the invited speakers. Margo, single, in her forties, was working her way through a doctoral degree as a self-employed consultant. She was presently conducting a study of the human service needs in our county under the aegis of the United Way. The study, like most, was suffering from inadequate funding and lack of paid staff. Margo had come to the meeting to recruit volunteers to assist with interviews.

Mumbling that I was an unemployed anthropologist, I introduced myself and offered to help. Margo grabbed my hand and pumped it enthusiastically. The incident proved to be a turning point; I worked as an independent consultant on that and several more research projects.

About a year later, I received a call regarding the United Way report. An attorney was representing a migrant worker on a death penalty case. The defendant had grown up during the sixties in one of the few barrios in our county. The United Way report had included the barrio. Margo had moved and I was the only person available familiar with the study. The attorney wanted to argue that the defendant's outlook, behavior, and opportunities were limited by his environment. I was to testify as an expert witness.

We agreed that I had to research the barrio's history. I was well experienced in such research. The main section of my doctoral dissertation is a community history of a small San Francisco Bay Area town. But this project had a strict time limit: three weeks. Besides, it was safe to work in the town only during daylight. Acquaintances from the United Way study told me that several community studies conducted during the past ten years were in the town library. From my doctoral fieldwork, I knew that small libraries often have local histories tucked away in locked cases. This library, too, had the anticipated papers by local residents. I also discovered a master's thesis based on research conducted by a human geographer. A gold mine of information, the thesis included a background history and detailed account of the town during the client's first 15 years of life. To get an inside view of the era, I scrutinized microfilms of the local newspapers. Finally, to verify that the defendant really had grown up in that town, I interviewed several longtime residents who had known him and his family.

My report to the attorney included everything I had discovered, including the fact that the defendant's grandmother had run a very successful bordello, that his mother had been a prostitute, and that his uncle was a major local drug dealer. Such facts, I believed, would have profoundly influenced the course of his life and limited his opportunities for success in the "straight" world.

I was surprised when the attorney's investigator called to say that the report was fine except for the piece on the family. The attorney thought the jury would find the information detrimental to his client. He wanted it kept out of the trial. Attorneys are trained to think strategically. One death penalty lawyer explained, "When attorneys investigate a criminal defendant's background they look for what can hurt them and how to 'bury' it."

When I investigate a case, I try to understand the defendant, her worldview, background, and relationships. Attorneys are not always sympathetic to complex arguments, but the more information juries have the more likely they are to rule for the defense. Oversimplifying the defendant's life makes her look pure but less credible.

After preparing the report, I had to testify in court. My first experience was nerve-wracking: I did not understand the dynamics of a criminal case, and no one explained them. The night before trial, I drove to a town 200 miles from home and met with the investigator in a motel room. When I asked questions about my role, she said the attorney would discuss that before I testified.

Five minutes before the case started, the attorney rushed up to me as I was standing nervously in the hall in my best "power" business suit. He spoke in a low voice, glancing around anxiously, obviously worried that the prosecution might hear him. Without waiting for me to speak, he smiled reassuringly and left. The two pieces of information I gleaned from him were: "The less you know the better" and "The D.A. will try to trip you up, but don't worry about it." Instantly, I started worrying: What did I know that I shouldn't? What was the district attorney going to do to me?

I walked into the courtroom, clutching four index cards with statistics on poverty, overcrowding, and lack of services in the community. I had left my report with the defense attorney because anything I took on the stand could be read by the district attorney and used in his cross-examination. The defense attorney established my credentials as an anthropologist and a researcher; I was qualified as an expert.

Direct examination then began. This was simple. The defense attorney asked me questions about my report which I answered to the best of my ability. Lulled into a false sense of security, I settled comfortably into the softness of the witness seat, just as the district attorney's cross-examination shattered my complacency.

Suddenly, I remembered that the defense attorney wanted the information about the defendant's family's involvement in drugs and prostitution to stay hidden. I held an ace! To my consternation, I felt myself blushing! I knew something that the district attorney would have given his eye teeth to know and for some unaccountable reason, I felt guilty about it.

Unaware of my shameful secret, the district attorney questioned me about my dog-eared cards, which he carefully examined. Then he asked me some questions about whether my newspaper research had revealed the existence of secret drug channels between the two towns. I said no, and the district attorney ended his cross-examination. Later I learned that the prosecutor had used me to make a point to the jury that the defendant was probably responsible for the local drug trade currently creating havoc in the town.

After the case, the investigator and I attended a conference on the death penalty. Realizing that there was work for anthropologists in death penalty litigation, I returned home with determination. First I went to the local public defender's office and applied for a job as "Investigator 1." As usual, my doctorate backfired and I was turned down. A friend from the American Civil Liberties Union (ACLU) gave me the name of a leading local defense attorney. His reaction was unenthusiastic: "What in heaven's name would I use an anthropologist for?!" I persuasively recited my prepared inventory of the tasks I could perform. Finally he suggested I call another attorney, who hired me to work on the penalty phase of an ongoing case. Since then, my work has come through word-of-mouth among the death penalty bar and through contacts made through my conference participation.

The California Death Penalty Statute

My work on death penalty cases is structured by the decisions of the United States Supreme Court in capital cases and by California state statute and case law. In the United States, executions have been a part of criminal law for the last 350 years. After peaking at 199 executions in 1935, the number declined steadily until, by the mid-1960s, executions had become rare. From 1967 through 1977, there was an unofficial moratorium on the death penalty, pending the resolution of various litigation challenging its constitutionality. By 1969, 11 states had either abolished the death penalty for all crimes or retained it for only a few offenses (such as murder of a law enforcement officer or murder by a prisoner already serving a life sentence). By 1986, 14 states and the District of Columbia had abolished the death penalty (Amnesty International 1989).[3]

In 1972, the United States Supreme Court decided *Furman v. Georgia,* invalidating all existing state death penalty laws because of their "arbitrary and capricious" application, due to the unlimited discretion afforded to the sentencing authority (juries or judges) in capital trials (Amnesty International 1989). But in 1976, the U.S. Supreme Court ruled in *Gregg v. Georgia* and related cases that the death penalty for murder was constitutional under a system of "guided discretion" as imposed under revised statutes in Georgia, Texas, and Florida. These statutes provided that: (1) The trial must be bifurcated: Guilt or innocence must be decided separately from sentence determination; (2) If a defendant is found guilty the separate sentencing hearing (the "penalty phase" of the trial) to determine the imposition of death or life imprisonment must consider aggravating and mitigating circumstances relating to both the crime and the offender.

California reinstated the death penalty in accordance with the *Gregg v. Georgia* requirements in 1977 through State Bill 155. On November 7, 1978, the California voters approved a still stronger death penalty law. Known as the Briggs Initiative, it appeared on the ballot together with Proposition 13, a conservative tax reform measure which attracted an unusually large number of voters to the polls. It is believed that the high conservative turnout on the tax measure influenced passage of the death penalty law which went into effect the following day as the Briggs Statute.

Codified as Section 190.2 of the California Penal Code, the Briggs Statute expands the special circumstances requiring either death or life imprisonment without parole.[4] If the jury finds a defendant guilty of murder involving any of the special circumstances, a sentence of either death in the gas chamber or life imprisonment without parole must be imposed. The same jurors who determine guilt convene a second time at the separate penalty phase of the trial to decide whether the sentence will be death *or* life. The Briggs Statute (codified as Section 190.3 of the California Penal Code) lists 11 factors that are deemed to aggravate or mitigate the crime and may be considered by the jury during the penalty phase. The Briggs Statute requires the jury to impose the death penalty if it finds that the aggravating circumstances outweigh the mitigating circumstances. If they do not, the jury must impose life imprisonment without parole.

The 11 aggravating and mitigating circumstances are:

1. The circumstances of the crime and the existence of any special circumstances.
2. The presence of or absence of criminal activity by the defendant which involved the use or attempted use of force or violence or the express or implied threat to use force or violence.

3. The presence or absence of any prior felony conviction.
4. Whether or not the defendant was under the influence of extreme mental or emotional disturbance.
5. Whether or not the victim was a participant in the defendant's homicidal conduct or consented to the homicidal act.
6. Whether or not the offense was committed under circumstances which the defendant reasonably believed to be a moral justification or extenuation for his conduct.
7. Whether or not the defendant acted under extreme duress or under the substantial domination of another person.
8. Whether or not at the time of the offense the capacity of the defendant to appreciate the criminality of his conduct or to conform his conduct to the requirements of law was impaired as a result of mental disease or defect, or the effects of intoxication.
9. The age of the defendant at the time of the crime.
10. Whether or not the defendant was an accomplice to the offense and his participation in the commission of the offense was relatively minor.
11. Any other circumstance which extenuates the gravity of the crime even though it is not a legal excuse for the crime.

Factor 1, the special circumstances surrounding the crime, is a particularly important weapon for the prosecution. By emphasizing these circumstances during the guilt phase of the trial, the prosecution has succeeded in convincing the jury that the defendant is guilty of murder—no longer a member of normal society. The jurors return for the penalty phase viewing the defendant in light of all they have heard during the guilt phase. Many strongly favor the death penalty. Harping on these same special circumstances, these same immediate brutal facts during the penalty phase, the prosecution reinforces the jurors' prejudice. Prosecution's goal is to make the crime appear "aggravated"—to prove that the defendant is a person of vicious nature who, having committed an ugly crime, deserves the gas chamber.

Defense counsel must persuade the jury that the defendant is not an inherently evil and sadistic animal but a human being. Defense focuses on explaining the defendant's character and behavior by presenting his life story. Factors 4, 6, 7, 8, and 9 place the crime in the broader context of the defendant's life and are important to the defense. Especially important is factor 11. This factor opens the door to admission of anything which "extenuates the gravity of the crime."[5] Defense counsel must prove that the crime was "mitigated" by circumstances.

One working definition of "mitigation," proposed by Craig Haney, defines it as anything that will lessen the juror's urge to punish with death (Dorman 1989:14). Opinions in capital cases have used similar definitions. See *Lockett v. Ohio*[6] ("any aspect of defendant's character . . ."); *Eddings v. Oklahoma*[7] (emotional disturbance and troubled upbringing); *Hitchcock v. Dugger*[8] (difficult circumstances of upbringing); *People v. Dyer*[9] ("A mitigating circumstance is any fact, condition or event which, as such does not constitute a justification or excuse for the offense in question, but which may be considered as an extenuating circumstance in determining the appropriateness of the death penalty.").

Through the testimony of lay and expert witnesses (sometimes including an anthropologist), the defense attorney presents mitigating evidence that (1) humanizes defendants, highlighting their good deeds and achievements; (2) stresses the disadvantages and difficulties they were born with and experienced throughout their lives; (3) highlights their good behavior while in jail awaiting trial; and (4) relates to the crime, such as feelings of lingering doubt or remorse. Selecting the appropriate mitigating evidence requires strategic legal thinking. Introduction of certain evidence, such as testimony about the defendant's good character, may open the door to otherwise inadmissable rebuttal testimony about the defendant's bad character. See, for example, *People v. Rodriguez.*[10] Also, factors which may be technically mitigating may be unimportant in relation to the crime or, like substance abuse, be regarded by some jurors as actually aggravating.

Constructing the Social History

My testimony as expert witness is usually based on my social history of the defendant's life, which provides the empirical data to support my conclusions about the influence of defendant's background. Doing the social history includes: (1) collection of evidence; (2) writing the social history; (3) analysis of the evidence for mitigating factors.

The social history focuses on two categories of mitigating evidence: the redeeming qualities of the defendant and the context and circumstances which have victimized the defendant.

As explained in *People v. Deere:*[11]

> The first broad category of mitigating evidence, the redeeming qualities of the defendant, is made up of facts that demonstrate the defendant has some positive character traits, has performed good deeds during his life, is valued by others, is remorseful, and has the potential to be a good prisoner. These facts can be discovered through interviews with the defendant, his family, friends, neighbors, school teachers, coaches, employers, social workers, ministers, prison employees and many other people who have some knowledge of the defendant.

As to the second category of mitigating evidence, *People v. Deere* explains:

> The defense must attempt to show that the defendant's capital crimes are humanly understandable in light of his past history and the unique circumstances affecting his formative development, that he is not solely responsible

> for what he is. . . . Counsel's demonstration that upbringing and other formative influences may have distorted the defendant's personality or led to his criminal behavior may spark in the sentencer the perspective or compassion conducive to mercy. [citations and quotations marks omitted]

On the witness stand, my expert testimony as a social anthropologist deals mainly with the mitigating factors associated with socioeconomic and cultural influences that have constrained or channelled the defendant's life. These can be categorized into three main groups:

1. The formal and informal social institutions in which the defendant has been involved, such as his family, his peer group, his neighbors, schools, clubs, fraternities, gangs, religious groups, and ethnic associations.
2. The economic and political groups and institutions that he has been involved with such as his employers, unions, the armed forces, children's protective services agencies, the juvenile justice system, probation departments, jails, prison systems, and hospitals.
3. The cultural values, community norms, and sociopolitical and religious beliefs that have influenced the defendant.

Often, discovery of favorable information regarding a client begins with an anecdote a witness relates. I discover further facts through interviews with a broad range of people and research in a variety of official records about the defendant, his family, his friends, the communities he lived in, and the many institutions that affected on his life.

Many mitigating factors emerge: dysfunctional family, child neglect and abuse, parental substance abuse, inadequate adult models, family violence, medical problems, migratory life-styles, poor socialization, inferior education, truancy, lack of job skills, gang values, neighborhood crime, economic hardship, institutional failure of the medical, educational, and criminal justice systems, racism, class discrimination, and cultural beliefs.

When first hired on a case, I discuss it briefly with the attorney who then sends me a selection of the information that has already been collected: police reports of the crime; interviews by the defense investigator with the defendant and witnesses; reports from other experts such as psychologists, psychiatrists, and child abuse experts; and public records from schools, hospitals, youth camps, probation officers, prisons, and social service agencies. Depending on the expertise of the defense investigator, the material the attorney sends me may be barely adequate or richly detailed. From it I construct a preliminary outline of the social history that chronologically documents the defendant's life. This outline exposes gaps in the information.

Using the preliminary outline, I discuss the deficiencies of the investigation with the attorney. If the deficiencies are serious and cannot be rectified by the investigator, I conduct the necessary research for the case myself, using the investigator whenever practicable. If the investigator has done a good job, I analyze the material for potential mitigating factors, using the above-mentioned categories as a guide, and brainstorm with the investigator about possible new evidence suggested by the material. I interview key informants located by the investigator and conduct additional documentary research to validate the information for myself.

Mitigating factors evident from the preliminary analysis may require further research or interpretation to explain their significance in the defendant's life. For example, school transcripts document the defendant's grades and absenteeism. By showing the relationship between changes in his grades, his truancy, and the onset of his mother's alcoholism, the defendant's eventual drop out from school and decline into delinquency can be explained to the jury. I use my expertise to plot and interpret these interrelationships and may use charts, diagrams, and other demonstrative evidence in explaining them to the jury.

The preliminary social history continues to act as a guide throughout the case, provoking questions and leading to further witnesses and records that can provide the answers. As I receive information, I incorporate it into the social history.

Sometimes evidence that will eventually be used in mitigation is not immediately apparent from the investigator's work and can only be tracked down through analysis of the data, deduction, further interviewing, and securing new documentary data. For example, evidence about child abuse is seldom revealed in a first round of interviewing; neither the abuser nor the abused willingly talks about it. In *"People v. Alison,"*[12] I strongly suspected that despite the defendant's contrary assertion, his father had been very abusive to him. To verify my suspicions, I contacted the local visiting nurse whose name I discovered on the school transcript. She had known the family and agreed to be interviewed. When I arrived at her home for the interview, I realized that she lived just down the road from the defendant's family. She was not just the visiting nurse; she was a neighbor whose children had attended school with the defendant. The nurse confirmed and later testified that she had visited defendant's home and that he had been the victim of child abuse. At that time, child abuse was often officially ignored and therefore there was no documentary record of our client's injuries.

In *"People v. Baez,"* I had similar suspicions about child neglect and abuse in the defendant's background, but the family had moved around too much for us to find anyone who remembered them. In this instance, the investigator looked for documentary evidence of the abuse in the Child Protective Service Agency records of the defendant's town. These records confirmed that the Agency had removed three children, including our client, from his mother's custody because of child neglect and abuse.

I use documents and charts to analyze the key pieces of information. I compose a family tree which highlights negative roles and events, such as "alcoholic," "substance abuser," "abortion," and "wife beater." I collect photographs of the defendant at different ages, of his family, and of the places he lived. I borrow trophies he has won, newspaper articles that mention him favorably, and certificates listing his achievements. I draw graphs tracing the decline of his school grades and attendance against major catastrophes in his life. All these "artifacts" of a defendant's life can be used during the penalty phase to enrich the testimony of lay and expert witnesses, educate the jury, and illustrate the final arguments to the attorney.

When I do my own research, I employ classic anthropological methods and concepts such as key informants, participant-observation, kinship systems, networks, and age-grades. I use them to find witnesses and information. I go into the defendant's neighborhood with someone he recommends. I participate in the everyday existence of the defendant's family, meeting people who can tell me what he was like at different periods during his life. Through his family members, friends, and neighbors, I learn the relationships, events, and institutions that have structured his life, the community norms that constrained his opportunities, and the cultural values and religious beliefs that have colored his worldview.

To understand the obstacles my client faced when he was growing up, I talk to residents of his community. In *"People v. Cash,"* I worked in the city of Compton in an area where drug dealers were being shot on the main street in broad daylight—much to the horror of my attorney friends who now refer to me behind my back as "that crazy anthropologist." Doing fieldwork in Compton, I learned from local storekeepers about the white-owned companies that moved out of the neighborhood, reducing it to a crime-ridden ghetto where unemployment for African-American youths is the norm. In *"People v. Dixon,"* I worked in south central Los Angeles where I listened to residents complain about the planning department's earthquake restrictions that require expensive renovation of dilapidated houses, such as the defendant once lived in, forcing their owners to abandon them. Again and again, in Watts and in Sacramento, in Long Beach and in San Diego, I listened to tales of racism or class discrimination that permeate every aspect of the community's life. Most of my clients are members of a minority group and their families are on welfare or struggling to make ends meet by working two minimum wage jobs.

Using the paper trail of records that has pursued my client, I research the formal and informal institutions through which he has passed: the schools, churches, community organizations such as the "Y" or the local Boys' Club, his gang, ethnic associations, his employers, the armed forces, juvenile hall, the probation department, jails, prisons, and hospitals. Interviews with people who knew him and others who understand the system clarify why he "failed" or why the institution failed him. In *"People v. Dixon,"* I traced the tragic saga of the youthful basketball star who was rescued from the ghetto only to fall victim to crack cocaine when he was not good enough to make it in basketball. At the end of my investigation I came to the realization that Dixon was a victim of an athletic system in which high school coaches built his hopes unrealistically high given his limited ability, but at the same time, with the best of intentions, allowed him to graduate without an education.

Finding and piecing together all these minutiae of evidence is like doing an enormous jigsaw puzzle: each little piece of information leads to other pieces. The completed puzzle is created by amassing everything possible about the defendant's life: the more pieces of evidence, the clearer the picture. As with all jigsaw puzzles, it takes time to find enough pieces to get a reliable picture. Sometimes the pieces are missing or have lost their shape over the years and do not fit the way they used to. The jigsaw puzzle is seldom complete, but the end product is the social history.

When time or funds have run out (for, as we all know, one never finishes collecting data) and the social history is as complete as it will ever be, I make a final analysis of the data. This provides the basis of my opinion about the case and outlines for the attorney the major mitigating evidence and themes on which he will build his case and final argument.

This analysis reveals dynamic relationships between supposedly unrelated factors. By combining in chronological order major events in the defendant's life with key incidents over which he had no control such as parents' divorce, moves, natural disasters, births, deaths, parental unemployment, wars, and mental breakdowns, it is possible to distinguish the major factors that influenced the course of the defendant's life. Patterns of behavior begin to emerge. As the story of his life unfolds in all its complexity, it becomes increasingly apparent that the defendant was not born a criminal but became one through a unique set of circumstances. This fact and the evidence to support it is the basis of my testimony during the penalty phase.

Acting as a Consulting Expert

When I am to testify as an expert witness my obligation to "tell the whole truth" when I am questioned and the prosecution's limited procedural right to "discover" what information and documents I have, may hamper my capacities as a researcher. If I learn too much I cannot testify. If I am told too little I cannot do honest and effective research.

Often, I can play a more useful role when I act as a nontestifying expert consultant. In my role as a consulting expert, I am brought into a case as a member of the defense team. Depending on the needs of the attorney, I perform some or all of the following tasks:

1. Work with the defense team to identify the themes and mitigating factors in a case

2. Compile a detailed social history of the client's life, analyzing and integrating data from investigators' reports and a wide variety of official records
3. Suggest investigations, interviews, and record searches
4. Coordinate the work of investigators
5. Conduct key interviews and institute record searches
6. Identify lay witnesses, interview them if necessary, and
7. Evaluate their potential strengths, weaknesses, and contributions to the case
8. Identify, locate, and interview experts necessary for a case
9. Analyze the strengths and weaknesses of different legal strategies in light of the facts disclosed by the social history research
10. Identify evidence and witnesses that can mitigate aggravating factors presented by the District Attorney
11. Assist the attorney with witness preparation
12. Assist the attorney with final arguments by:
    a. analyzing jury profiles
    b. outlining the mitigating arguments I believe are best suited to appeal to particular jurors, and
    c. pointing out factors that might alienate some or all jurors.

I am also able to use my anthropological expertise to help the defense team communicate across cultural barriers. My training and experience in interviewing sometimes enable me to elicit information lost to the investigator's more direct approach. For example, in a recent case I asked the investigator to question the defendant's sister about her alcoholic father. I suspected the man of abusing his daughter sexually and felt this might have had a profound effect on my client's attitude toward women. I thought that if the investigator talked to her about her father's alcoholism the conversation might lead to talk about sexual abuse. The information would be valuable to the psychologist who would be testifying as an expert witness on behalf of our client. Although the investigator knew what I wanted, she returned from the interview empty handed.

Convinced that the client's sister knew more than she was telling, I arranged to meet her at a place of her own choosing. I knew that if she could control the interview as much as possible she might eventually trust me enough to talk openly to me. We met in a noisy, crowded Denny's near the freeway. When I arrived I had a splitting headache and was finding it difficult to hear her. Some three hours later, tired of hearing all the stories I had already read in the investigator's interview reports, I was about to end the interview when she said to me, "Well, I might as well tell you, I decided I was going to before we met, if you were an O.K. person." She then related a lurid account of how she was sexually abused at the age of 7 by her father, the man who had told my client at the age of 10 that he was going to take him out and shoot him. As she told me her story she wept quietly. Wiping the tears away from my own eyes, I held her hands across the table, grateful for her generosity in sharing with me a fact that might tip the scales in favor of her brother's life.

Through the investigator or my own interviews, I learn about each potential witness's strengths and weaknesses and the contributions and problems he or she can contribute to the case. I discuss these with the attorney and help select the best witness to present a specific piece of evidence.

At the time of the trial I assist in coordinating the witnesses. I can facilitate the "cultural translation" of the defendant's culture into the culture of the court. Very often I act as an interpreter between the two parties, explaining and mediating between them. In a recent case, members of the defendant's family were making a number of excuses about testifying: it was clear they were frightened and reluctant to come to court. The attorney assumed that this problem could be overcome by issuing them a subpoena. This alienated them further. After a lengthy discussion with each witness, I learned they believed that the client's mother could commit "hoo-doo" on them if they testified about her mental condition. They had been too embarrassed to tell the attorney. After I convinced the attorney of their beliefs, we solved the problem by assigning an investigator whom the witnesses liked and trusted to keep the mother busy while we brought them into the court.

Sometimes I also translate from the defendant's culture into another professional culture with which the court is familiar—that of the mental health professions. I am also able to locate other expert witnesses in specific areas of psychology, psychiatry, addiction, child abuse, and other fields who can testify on the effects of the traumatic experiences I have discovered in researching the defendant's life. Through my reading and my contacts with local universities and other attorneys, I am able to locate experts who are able to testify to specific features of the defendant's background or to his personality and behavior. For example, in *"People v. Dixon,"* several family witnesses testified to the substance abuse of the client's mother. To show the impact her behavior had on our client, we used an expert on the behavior of children of alcoholics to explain how the self-defeating behavior our client had displayed throughout his adult years was a survival strategy he developed during his chaotic childhood. A jury that may be predisposed to condemn a defendant's whole cultural background along with the defendant may respond with empathic leniency when the same cultural context is explained as a dysfunctional system that has produced psychopathology in the defendant.

At the close of trial I assist the defense attorney with her final arguments. Based on the social history, I outline the mitigating arguments of the case, incorporating testimony from lay and expert witnesses. I discuss these arguments with the attorney, evaluating them for their applicability to the particular jury, the defense attorney, and the district attorney, and brainstorming different ways in which they can be presented. Each attorney has a different style, but every one I have worked with goes through an emotional beating at the end of the trial waiting for the jury to pass their verdict. Some attorneys can only handle one death penalty case in their lives. Others continue to work for the outcasts of our society, living with the snide comments of their friends and neighbors who "just can't understand how you can defend someone like that."

Notes

Furman v. Georgia, 408 U.S. 238 (1972).

[2]Gregg v. Georgia, 428 U.S. 153 (1976).

[3]The trend toward abolition was worldwide. In 1971 the United Nations General Assembly adopted a resolution affirming the desirability of abolishing capital punishment in all countries in order to fully guarantee the right to life, as provided for in Article 3 of the Universal Declaration of Human Rights. As of May 1986, almost all the Western democracies had abolished the death penalty: 28 had abolished it entirely, and 18 retained the death penalty only for exceptional crimes such as those under military law or committed during wartime (Amnesty International 1989).

[4]Under section 190.2 of the California Penal Code, special circumstances now include: Intentional murder for financial gain; conviction for more than one murder at this trial or previously; murder through destructive device, bomb, or explosive recklessly planted or concealed in any place or structure or recklessly mailed or delivered; murder to avoid or escape arrest or escape from custody; murder of a peace officer, a federal law enforcement officer or agent, or a fireman, in performance of his duties or in retaliation for performance of his duties; murder of a witness to a crime to prevent her testimony or in retaliation for such testimony; murder of a present or former prosecutor or assistant prosecutor, a judge or former judge, or an elected or appointed official of the federal or any state or local government to prevent performance of duty or in retaliation for having performed it; murder that is especially heinous, atrocious, or cruel, manifesting exceptional depravity (a conscienceless or pitiless crime, unnecessarily torturous to the victim); murder committed in the commission, accomplice, attempted commission, or immediate flight from the felonies of robbery, kidnapping, rape, sodomy, child molestation, oral copulation, burglary, arson, or train wrecking; and intentional murder involving the infliction of torture or through the administration of poison.

[5]The American Heritage Dictionary defines "extenuate" as "1. To lesson or attempt to lessen the magnitude of [an offense or guilt] by providing partial excuses; and 2. To cause to appear less serious or blameworthy."

[6]Lockett v. Ohio, 438 U.S. 586, 604 (1978).

[7]Eddings v. Oklahoma, 455 U.S. 104, 112 (1982).

[8]Hitchcock v. Dugger, 107 S. Ct. 1821 (1987).

[9]People v. Dyer, 45 Cal. 3d 26 (1988).

[10]People v. Rodriguez, 42 Cal. 2d 730, 702–769, 726 P.2d 113 (1986).

[11]People v. Deere, (1985).

[12]To protect informant and client confidentiality where statements about cases have not resulted in published opinions, the case names used are pseudonyms. Such case names appear in quotation marks.

Inquiry and Advocacy: Attorney-Expert Collaboration in the Political Asylum Process

Lynn Alvarez and James Loucky

Expert witnesses, by definition, assist the trier of fact in a court case to understand the evidence or to determine a fact in issue.[1] Anthropologists have been instrumental in Indian claims litigation (Dobyns 1978; Joans 1984; Lurie 1955; Stewart 1973) and other cases (Hopper 1990). There is an increasing awareness that they can also serve the needs of immigrants facing deportation or exclusion from the United States.[2]

The anthropologist is especially important in immigration cases where the respondent is seeking political asylum in the United States because the anthropologist can successfully tackle four institutional obstacles: (1) political interference; (2) cultural insensitivity; (3) lack of impartiality; and (4) lack of information. This article examines the crucial role of the expert anthropologist in the context of several political asylum cases involving Maya from Huehuetenango, Guatemala.

A respondent facing deportation proceedings who fears returning to his or her country may apply for political asylum.[3] If this form of relief is granted, the respondent may remain in the United States and eventually become a permanent resident.[4] Although a deportation proceeding is not criminal in nature, the consequences of being deported can often mean death. As a result, a person facing deportation is accorded substantial due process including the right to present evidence and witnesses, to be represented by counsel, and to inspect evidence introduced by the Immigration and Naturalization Service (INS) against him or her.[5]

Most of the cases presently pending before the immigration courts in Los Angeles, San Diego, and El Centro, California, involve indigent Central Americans who lack the resources to obtain the assistance of an expert. While the issues presented by this case are typical, the presence of an attorney (Lynn Alvarez), documentation, and an expert (James Loucky) are unusual.

The Asylum Claim

The cases reported here involved ten indigenous Guatemalan respondents. Most of them spoke the Maya language of Kanjobal[6] and all were from the department (state) of Huehuetenango, in northwest Guatemala. The cases were heard consecutively, with the same expert testimony offered into evidence in each case. The immigration judge chose to combine the cases in this fashion because similar issues were raised.

Each respondent had a different story but all shared a common ethnicity and cultural history which were central to the "present fear" of returning to Guatemala.

The attorney provided the expert with copies of the asylum applications in each case. The expert then took the unusual step of travelling to Guatemala to obtain recent and specific evidence to submit to the court. He spoke to the respondents' family members still remaining in Guatemala and to other villagers who were able to give an account of life in Huehuetenango before and after the respondents' flight. In addition, the expert was able to obtain clippings from local newspapers that are not available in the United States.

Guatemala is rich in physical resources and cultural diversity, with indigenous people comprising over half of its eight million inhabitants. But it also has one of the worst human rights records in the world. One military government after another has maintained the most inequitable land distribution system in Latin America. Health and living standards are abysmal, particularly for the Maya population who have endured continuous discrimination and repression.

When social tensions escalated into civil war in the late 1970s, the military's response was quick and brutal. It moved in mass into the rural area in the early 1980s, following few rules of war as it applied a "Guatemalan solution" (i.e., indiscriminate massacres and exemplary torture) to popular reform as well as the growing insurgency. By the army's own account, 440 villages were destroyed in scorched earth campaigns. An entire generation of community leaders and youth was decimated. Those who could, fled; over half a million Guatemalans, many of them Indians, are believed to have arrived in Mexico and the United States since 1980.

The Huehuetenango region became a stronghold of guerrilla activity in opposition to the Guatemalan army. Suspecting all indigenous Maya in that area of supporting the guerrillas, the Guatemalan army initiated a campaign of castigation and killing, targeting Indian communities as well as the elusive guerrilla units. Without distinguishing between combatants and civilians, the army burned to the ground entire Kanjobal villages. Escaping refugees recounted decapitations, machine-gunning of children, rape, and the destruction of crops and animals. The aggressive military campaign was followed by a systematic counterinsurgency program to control the indigenous population through obligatory service in "civil patrols" and restrictions on travel and work.

Although a civilian president was elected in 1985, Guatemala continues to have one of the worst human rights records in the Western hemisphere. The number of political killings is lower than in the early 1980s, but the apparatus of military control has been extended and strengthened. An elaborate system of army bases, model villages, and army-directed civil defense patrols ensures a permanent military presence and close monitoring of civilian activity throughout the highlands where the Kanjobal live (Americas Watch 1988).

Each new wave of repression at the hands of the military or the guerrillas directly affected the respondents. Some testified that the guerrillas sometimes used force and intimidation to obtain support and cooperation from the villagers. Pablo,[7] one of the respondents, was severely beaten and had one eye permanently damaged by the guerrillas because he refused to cooperate. The guerrillas also attempted to forcibly conscript several respondents into their ranks. Although they wished to remain neutral, the respondents were clearly pressured from both sides. Villagers who refused to support the guerrillas would be accused of favoring the military; at the same time, the military considered most Kanjobal to be guerrilla pawns.

In 1982 the Guatemalan army began to form civil patrols in the respondents' villages, appointing civil patrol commanders from within the community and establishing an extensive network of informers. Backed by the army, commanders were responsible for denouncing people for supporting the guerrillas and for mobilizing civil patrol and other labor duties. To this day, anyone denounced by a commander faces consequences ranging from double patrol duty to death. Some respondents reported punishment in the form of beatings and confinement in holes filled with freezing water. Jacob's brother-in-law and cousin were killed by the army for aiding the guerrillas. Domingo reported that in 1982 the military rounded up Kanjobal Indians who had allegedly supported the guerrillas, forced them to dig their own graves, and summarily executed them in public. The military arrested Pablo's sister because her husband was suspected of being a guerrilla collaborator. She died two months after her release.

Most respondents reported being forced to patrol for 24 hours at a time as often as twice a week. They were not fed or compensated in any way for this service, which the Guatemalan constitution stipulates is voluntary. Respondents reported being required to repair roads and do other uncompensated hard labor for the army, often for days at a time. They were also sent out unarmed to hunt guerrillas in the surrounding mountains. The military prevented the Kanjobal from traveling outside their villages without the written permission of the commander. This restriction imposed real hardship on people who earn their living largely through agriculture and who need to visit plots of land located far from the village and sell their produce in the nearest town or city.

Furthermore, respondents feared that escalating guerrilla activity toward the end of the 1980s would mean more massacres like those that occurred earlier in the decade. As a result, they fled Guatemala even though the act of leaving the country further branded them as "subversives." In the United States they applied for political asylum before an immigration judge after the INS arrested and threatened to deport them.

Standard for Granting Political Asylum

To receive a grant of political asylum, the immigration judge must find that the respondents have either been "victims of past persecution"[8] or have a subjectively and objectively reasonable[9] "well-founded fear of persecution" because of their race, political opinion, religion, nationality, or membership in a social group[10] should they return to Guatemala.

Even if the judge finds that a respondent possesses a well-founded fear of persecution, he or she can exercise discretion to deny asylum if the negative factors in the case outweigh the favorable factors.[11] But if it is established that the respondent is "more likely than not" to be persecuted, the judge must withhold deportation under section 243(h) of the Immigration and Nationality Act. The judge also has the task of determining if respondents are credible. If they are found not to be credible, asylum will not be granted.

The respondents in this case argued that the massacres by the military in the early 1980s and its continued use of compulsory civil patrols, obligatory sweeps, forced labor, and travel restrictions were forms of persecution directed against them because of their race and imputed political opinions. In the context of their asylum claims, the respondents belonged to the Maya Indian race. The anthropologist described the physical and cultural similarities shared by the Kanjobal-speaking Maya. Their physical appearance, unique naming system, and language made them easily recognizable as a separate group. Because they had provided food and shelter to the guerrillas, albeit by force, pro-guerrilla political opinions were imputed to them by the Guatemalan government. The respondents introduced documentary evidence to corroborate their claims.

The anthropologist whose observations in Guatemala had confirmed the practices the respondents complained of, testified before they took the stand. His testimony brought the asylum applications and corroborating documentary evidence to life. Most important, however, it mitigated the detrimental effects of significant institutional obstacles. As a result, the respondents were granted asylum in the United States.

Institutional Biases

From a human rights standpoint, many Guatemalans, and Maya Indians in particular, merit asylum in the United States. However, several institutional biases weigh against them (Loucky 1989). In the Kanjobal cases, the testimony of the anthropologist was crucial in overcoming these biases.

Political Interference by State Department Advisory Opinions

In all asylum cases the immigration judge is required to mark into evidence an opinion from the Bureau of Human Rights and Humanitarian Affairs (BHRHA) of the U.S. Department of State.[12] The opinion typically consists of a form letter which does not address the facts raised by the respondents' claims. In these cases none of the advisory opinions from the BHRHA recommended asylum.

This initial requirement creates the first institutional obstacle respondents had to overcome: political interference from the State Department. Not only do judges rely on the State Department opinions, they also consult State Department country reports as primary sources of information on the human rights conditions in a country. The judges place great weight on the opinions rendered by the State Department, which is unabashedly more concerned with United States political and foreign policy situations than respondents' needs (Fagen 1984).

In the respondents' cases the State Department acknowledged some "violence" in Guatemala but opined that conditions had changed significantly under a "freely elected civilian government," making it safe for the respondents to return to Guatemala. Given the close ties between the US government and the present Guatemalan government, to acknowledge the validity of respondents' claims would have been politically imprudent.[13]

The expert anthropologist was able to respond to this political interference. The State Department often obtains its information indirectly from interested government sources and government-controlled media (Americas Watch 1987). The expert was able to convince the judge that his differing opinion was based on a thorough, objective, and lengthy exploration into the subject. He refuted the contentions that it was now safe to return to Guatemala and that human rights had vastly improved. He explained that although a civilian is president, the military maintains control of Guatemala. Given a choice between authoritative in-person testimony and the politically motivated State Department opinion the judge chose the expert's opinion.

Cultural Insensitivity

The second obstacle is cultural insensitivity. The judge, the attorneys, and the immigration court system as a whole are securely planted in Western culture. The respondents, on the other hand, came from a culture so different that a cultural interpreter was required. The anthropologist assumed this role.

Before arriving in the United States, the respondents married, raised families, and farmed the way their ancestors have done for hundreds of years. Their ancient culture had been relatively isolated from Western influences for centuries. Western notions of courtroom behavior were unknown to them. The anthropologist, sharing his years of Guatemalan experience with the court, was able to bridge the gap in understanding by sensitizing the judge and attorneys to Kanjobal culture. The anthropologist laid out the physical and cultural factors unique to the respondents, helping to explain why the Kanjobals had been targeted by both the guerrillas and the army. He also elucidated their reluctance to express emotions and inability to recall dates and details.

Clarifying the respondents' behavior and motivation enhances their credibility in the eyes of the judge (Kalin 1986; Kot 1988). Conversely, misunderstood gestures, expressions, emotions, and speech patterns promote distrust. For instance, the respondents' lack of eye contact with the judge and their indirect answers to questions were intended by them as signs of respect. Without the anthropologist to explain this, the judge might have interpreted such behavior as attempts to deceive and found the respondents not credible. The judge's perception of courtroom demeanor is important because granting asylum depends on a subjective component (that the applicant genuinely fears persecution), as well as the objective component (a reasonable possibility that he or she would be persecuted). Because Guatemalans usually lack material evidence of persecution, success hinges largely on their credibility. This makes the expert's role in explaining cultural differences such as time reckoning or timidity in the courtroom even more valuable.

Lack of Impartiality

In all deportation cases, the burden is on the respondent to prove that he or she is eligible for the relief sought.[14] But the judges and the administrative appellate court that reviews their decisions often place additional burdens of proof on the respondent that are not warranted by the statutes or Supreme Court decisions (Anker 1990). Many judges formerly worked for the INS or the government, prosecuting deportations, and all answer to the U.S. Attorney General.[15] By definition then, the immigration courts are not an independent judiciary because their employer has a stake in the outcome of deportation cases.

Recently the government acknowledged such bias in the settlement of *American Baptist Churches v. Thornburgh* (ABC).[16] The lawsuit alleged that the U.S. government had discriminated against nationals of El Salvador and Guatemala in the adjudication of their asylum applications. As part of the settlement, the government agreed to provide new asylum interviews for all Salvadoran and Guatemalan applicants. These new interviews were to be conducted by trained asylum officers who had been instructed to disregard ideological, foreign policy, and border enforcement considerations in deciding whether the applicant had a well-founded fear of persecution. Acknowledging past bias is one step toward correcting the lack of impartiality in the system.

Despite the great strides made through the *ABC* settlement, lack of impartiality persists in the immigration court. The judge is the trier of fact and law in asylum cases. The rules of evidence are more relaxed in deportation hearings than in court trials. In this informal atmosphere, lack of impartiality is dangerous. Often judges take over the prosecutorial role. The presence of an expert witness however, can formalize the proceedings because the judge and the attorneys know they are being observed by an outside professional. Furthermore, since experts rarely testify in such hearings, having one appear indicates that the applicant and counsel believe the case is strong and worthy of appeal if the judge denies asylum. The prospect of being reviewed on appeal injects an additional incentive for the judge to conduct a fair and impartial hearing.

Lack of Information on the Country or Claim Presented

The fourth institutional obstacle which confronts a respondent seeking asylum is the judge's lack of information about the respondent's home country. Although judges are expected to hear cases from respondents of all nationalities and make detailed findings they receive little professional training about human rights conditions around the world. It becomes the respondent's job to educate the court.

In the context of the immigration court nothing is as effective an educational tool as the live testimony of an expert witness, especially an anthropologist. In this case, the anthropologist was able to put respondents' fear in a historical context. On his trip to Guatemala to contact some of respondents' neighbors and families, he anticipated and sought answers to some of the judge's concerns and questions. For instance, the judge wanted to know whether the respondents would be safe in Guatemala outside of the department of Huehuetenango. The anthropologist explained that the Kanjobal's distinctive features, mannerisms, language, and naming system made them conspicuous in other regions. The judge was also concerned about the involuntary nature of civil patrols and work projects. The anthropologist was able to explain why civil patrols, which exist elsewhere in Guatemala, were especially onerous to the Kanjobal. He also testified that involuntary labor was enforced in a discriminatory manner. This information persuaded the judge that many Kanjobal were singled out because of their imputed affiliation with the guerrillas.

In the case of Guatemala, counterinsurgency operations have amounted to a "hidden war" carried out largely in isolated regions and beyond the attention of journalists. An unfavorable State Department letter may be a judge's only source of background information. Written materials that are available, such as newspaper articles, reports from human rights organizations, and scholarly studies, are not designed with the immigration court in mind. Although publications by organizations such as Amnesty International and Human Rights Watch can be made available to the immigration court, the judge usually doesn't see them until the day of the trial and they are often too voluminous to read on such short notice.

As an anthropologist, the expert was able to address all of the judge's questions. He could educate the judge on the racial and ethnic classification of the Kanjobal Indians and their geographical distribution. He could explain how the history of cultural conflict in Guatemala created the power relationships between the Kanjobal and the white latino minority and how it continues to affect their present reality. The anthropologist's detailed information was imperative to the judge's ability to make an informed decision.

Dynamics of Counsel-Expert Interaction

Because the asylum process involves merging cultural and legal considerations, anthropological knowledge is a unique and potentially critical element in preparing and presenting asylum cases. This case shows how collaboration between anthropologist and attorney may be enhanced.

Qualifications

In political asylum proceedings, expert witnesses may be called to speak to the applicability of international law, to provide a psychological evaluation, or—in the case of most anthropologists—to clarify in-country conditions. Standards for admissibility of expert testimony vary depending on the particulars of each case, inclinations of the judge, and a scholar's qualifications. However, the nature of anthropological work, the length of time spent in the field, positions and publications, consulting done in other contexts, and the means by which researchers keep abreast of conditions in areas where they have worked are all relevant to expertise.

Insofar as anthropologists recognize the complexity of human behavior and the intricacies of cultural phenomena, they tend to be modest about their expertise beyond the world of the village or groups with whom they have lived and done fieldwork. Nevertheless, anthropologists may be uniquely qualified to be expert witnesses in the context of immigration proceedings precisely because they speak with people of diverse backgrounds and develop understanding of the reasoning and emotions that motivate them.[17] In this case, the anthropologist's knowledge of conditions in Guatemala stemmed from traditional ethnographic experience in that country, applied research with indigenous Guatemalans settled in the United States, and two trips in the late 1980s specifically to investigate the human rights situation in Huehuetenango.

The anthropologist, working with the attorney, may prepare an affidavit (sworn statement), which is an invaluable way to outline qualifications, document years when work was conducted in the respondent's country, and demonstrate familiarity with the facts of the case and with the area from which the applicant originates. A well constructed affidavit with numbered paragraphs saves the court's time and may encourage the INS to stipulate to the anthropologist's expertise. A signed affidavit that speaks to the particulars of a case may sometimes be admitted as evidence in cases where an expert cannot testify in person.

Cross-Preparation

For the anthropologist, the importance of advance preparation cannot be overemphasized. Studying the respondent's declaration and the State

Department advisory opinion and discussing the facts of the case with counsel, enables an expert to learn how counsel intends to build the case and permits inclusion of anthropological insights to help establish it. For example, the anthropologist was able to anticipate and allay the court's fear of thousands of Kanjobal Maya flooding the border by asserting that not all Kanjobal would be equally subject to persecution on return. Direct observation and extensive interviews enabled the anthropologist to elaborate on how personal involvement in community organizations, place of origin (and its reputation for "subversive" loyalties), age, sex, and actual or imputed political opinion were some of the factors bearing on potential risks to individual Kanjobal.

Preparation also ensures the inclusion of vital issues and information. Counsel may be unaware of documentation about a respondent's country of origin that may help substantiate claims for which the respondent lacks physical corroboration. For example, the anthropologist described how Kanjobal could be tracked by the sophisticated urban surveillance network in Guatemala, showing that relocation within Guatemala would not guarantee safety.

Courtroom Culture

Most potential expert witnesses are neophytes in the political asylum process and court procedure. Knowing the process makes testifying as an expert easier (cf. Sklar, Hing, and Silverman 1985). Before testifying, an expert witness may have to undergo a preliminary investigation to establish areas in which the court will accept his or her expertise. An expert witness must then be sufficiently prepared to be convincing within this area of expertise. During direct examination, the expert may be asked not only to testify to facts observed directly but also to draw conclusions or posit opinions (for example, on the consequences of hypothetical circumstances for individuals).

During cross examination, the INS questions the expert to bring out propositions favorable to its case or impugn the validity of facts already testified to. The expert is more effective answering questions precisely and succinctly (often with a simple yes or no) than delivering the lengthy commentary typical of much academic discourse.

Framing questions and answers properly allows the witness to exercise control over the "flow" of testimony. In the Kanjobal case, the anthropologist deliberately understated the history of massive violence experienced by indigenous Guatemalans during the 1980s because the situation was so horrible as to seem exaggerated when reported fully. The expert also pointed out that, if deported, Kanjobal refugees would face considerable risk not only because their flight labeled them politically suspect but also because those remaining feared that the refugees' return would endanger everyone. In addition, because experiencing freedom and adapting to new circumstances outside Guatemala changes the refugees, it would be very difficult for them to successfully reenter a system of subtle yet comprehensive military control requiring silence and regimented conformity.

Conclusion

Anthropologists contemplating the unfamiliar turf of the courtroom may fear that their objectivity will be compromised if they do their best for their clients. Like everyone else in the courtroom, a witness is under an obligation to tell the truth. However, this does not mean that witnesses are expected to be wholly impartial. Indeed, being forthright about what is opinion and what is fact and about what one does or does not know enhances the expert's credibility.

Academic modes of inquiry are indeed distinct from those pursued by attorneys and there are problems using expert opinions. Yet, there is considerable overlap in the goals of applied research and legal advocacy. Anthropological testimony can be particularly invaluable in an asylum proceeding. In a particular case, expert testimony establishes a strong record should appeal become necessary. More generally, expert testimony can educate both counsel and the judge, sensitizing them for future cases. With sufficient careful research and interactive education during case preparation, collaboration can be successful.

Notes

[1]Federal Rules of Evidence 702.

[2]For purposes of this article, immigrants in deportation or exclusion proceedings are referred to collectively as "respondents."

[3]Immigration and Nationality Act section 208(a), 8 U.S.C. section 1158(a) (1992).

[4]Immigration and Nationality Act section 209, 8 U.S.C. section 1159 (1992).

[5]Immigration and Nationality Act section 292, 8 U.S.C. section 1362 (1992); Immigration and Nationality Act section 242 (b), U.S.C. section 1252 (b) (1992).

[6]Although spelled "Q'anhob'al" according to recent national-level changes in orthography, the spelling in use at the time of trial has been retained here.

[7]Pseudonyms are used to protect the individual and his or her family still living in Guatemala.

[8]I.N.S. v. Cardoza Fonseca, 767 F.2d 1448 (9th Cir. 1985), *aff'd,* 480 U.S. 421 (1987).

[9]Rodriguez-Rivera v. INS, 848 F.2d 998 (9th Cir. 1988).

[10]Immigration and Nationality Act section 243 (h), 8 U.S.C. section 1253(h) (1992).

[11]Immigration and Nationality Act section 208(a), 8 U.S.C. section 1158(a) (1992).

[12]8 C.F.R. section 208.11 (c).

[13]Evidence of the strong political bias against granting asylum to applicants from countries considered to be allies is seen in fiscal year 1987 figures, where only 3.8% of Guatemalans won asylum, compared to 83.9% of Nicaraguans granted asylum in the same year.

[14]McMullen v. INS, 658 F.2d 1312 (9th Cir. 1981), *petition for review denied,* 788 F.2d 591 (9th Cir. 1986).

[15]Immigration and Nationality Act section 103(a), 8 U.S.C. section 1103(a) (1982).

[16]American Baptist Churches v. Thornburgh, Civ. No. C-85-3255 RFP.

[17]Compare the "expertise" presumed by journalists who file stories from hotels of capital cities or by foreign officials who conduct fact-finding missions of a few hours or days of duration.

III. A Legal Field Guide for the Expert Anthropologist

Randy Frances Kandel

Becoming an expert in a court case raises many questions. What should I say? How should I say it? What can I be made to reveal or asked to conceal? How can I best make anthropological ideas intelligible to judge or jury? Can I be forced to compromise my confidentiality with my informants or turn over my fieldnotes?

This outline is intended as a field guide to lawsuits as an anthropological expert is likely to encounter them. This guide refers to the Federal Rules of Evidence and the Federal Rules of Civil Procedure. These rules, developed by the U.S. federal judiciary, under the authority of the Federal Rules Enabling Act,[1] are laws which govern respectively the admission of testimony at trial and the conduct of civil litigation. The Rules of Evidence apply in both civil and criminal trials. Most state courts have similar rules. Rules of procedure differ more among the various state court systems. The rules of criminal procedure are different and generally allow for more limited and specific "discovery" (pretrial exchange of information) between the parties. Criminal procedure rules also differ from state to state.

Ethical Approaches: To Advocate or Educate?

As the articles in this volume suggest, "[T]here are few roles that confront conscientious anthropologists with more serious scholarly and ethical problems than those posed by their appearance as expert witnesses" (Rosen 1977:555). Only a bare framework for analysis of the issues that confront an expert anthropologist can be indicated here. In general, they stem from two sources. First are the changes in loyalty, obligation, and task which arise as one moves from the role of researcher, to that of paid consultant for a party to litigation, to a sworn witness before a court. Second are the differences in explanation between anthropology and law, and between academic analysis and witnesses' testimony.

Most anthropologists who are asked to be experts have had longstanding prior personal and research relationships with the people, cultures, or communities who are parties or subjects in the case. The Principles of Professional Responsibility of the American Anthropological Association (AAA Principles) (American Anthropological Association 1971) state that "anthropologists' first responsibility is to those whose lives and cultures they study." Their "physical, social, and emotional safety and welfare" are professional concerns and their wishes regarding publicity or confidentiality are to be respected.

Conflict inevitably arises and must be resolved whenever the people studied and the parties to a case are not identical; that is, when one's expertise is sought in a case by or against a particular individual or by a "corporate" entity such as a tribal council or community organization which the anthropologist believes does not represent the interest of all; or by a "class" which is not representative of the group studied but is certified by the court as having a common legal concern. Conflict also occurs where members of the group are allied on opposite sides of the case or may suffer and benefit differentially from its prosecution. Confidentiality issues become acute because of the court's power to force disclosure of relevant materials that the anthropologist holds confidential. Before accepting work as an expert one should answer to one's own ethical satisfaction the question: To what extent should or may my testimony be limited by professional confidences owed to others outside the scope of the litigation?

As practitioner anthropologists know well, a second set of ethical issues revolves around the position of consultant. The professional obligations placed upon a practitioner are summarized in paragraph 3 of the National Association of Practicing Anthropologists' Ethical Guidelines for Practitioners which states in part: "To our employers we owe competent, efficient, fully professional skills and techniques, timely performance of our work and communication of our findings and recommendations in understandable, non-jargonistic language."

The conflict created by the tension between obligations to one's informants and obligations to one's employer, which occurs in all practitioner contexts, is further complicated in litigation because of the range of legitimate ethical stances on the extent to which an expert hired by a party should be an "advocate" or a neutral "educator" of the court. The expert is most commonly expected to become a part of the litigation "team"—sharing in case strategy, emphasizing (without distortion) those facts and ideas which are most helpful to the client, and assisting in scripting the cross-examination of party experts for the client's adversary. However, this is not the only respectable stance. Further, each position raises corollary questions. For example, in an adversary system of justice that expects partisan experts, is an "educative" role less than fair to the client and the case? Or, if testimony is expressed in the strong, clear, direct, "non-jargonistic" language that is effective in the courtroom, will it fail to communicate the qualifications and limitations on one's expert opinion consistent with academic honesty or an "educative" role? Before becoming an expert one should resolve the answer to the following question: Is the purpose of my testimony to "advocate" for a client by marshalling the best opinion possible based upon an honest, professional evaluation of the facts or to "educate" the court through an opinion balancing all sides?

An additional set of issues is raised by the way in which one's commitment to political, moral, or legal issues (such as the abolition of the death penalty) or the advance of anthropological knowledge and theory may or should impact upon one's responsibilities as an expert. To what extent should the differences in fact, explanation, purpose, and understanding between law and anthropology affect the use of anthropological theory by an expert witness? Is it obligatory or advisable to disclose one's theoretical stance (if one is even conscious of one's stance) in the same way that one discloses the limits and sources of one's data? Is such disclosure helpful to the normative judgments the law must make or to the progress of anthropology? Should courts of law serve as a cauldron for anthropological debate, or should anthropological input into the legal process be restricted to the more moderate paths of policy formulation?[2]

Each of these questions requires a whole volume and entails a deeply personal choice. The reader is referred to the discussions by anthropologists: Hopper 1990; Rosen 1977, 1979; Stewart 1979; and members of our sister disciplines (for example, McCloskey, Egeth, and McKenna 1986).

The remainder of this chapter assumes that the reader has been hired by a party as an expert and will participate as part of the litigation team in the strategic organization and presentation of testimony to the extent consistent with the honesty and integrity required by a court of law and the discipline of anthropology.[3] This is not the only possible stance of an expert witness, but I believe it is the one most usual and expected in practice; the one contemplated by the rules of discovery and evidence of most U.S. jurisdictions, and the one most compatible with the NAPA Guidelines and the AAA Principles.

Within this framework, ethical conflicts will still frequently arise: between one's obligations to the people and culture studied and one's commitments to the case and client; between the role of advocate one's client may expect one to play and one's commitment to fairly educate the court; and between the needs of the case, the client, and the people studied and one's own commitment to legal change and the progress of anthropology.

This chapter suggests ways in which some of those conflicts may be resolved within the structure of litigation. Sometimes they cannot. It is assumed that where an anthropologist's honest, objective testimony is not helpful to a party, or where scholarly questions or concerns for one's people beyond the scope of the case will significantly interfere with one's ability to testify, the anthropologist will not accept the case or will terminate the work. Again, I believe this view is consistent both with the mainstream of ethical practice and paragraph 3 of the NAPA Guidelines, which states in part:

> When, at any time during the course of work performance, the demands of the employer require or appear to require you to violate the ethical standards of our profession, we have the responsibility to clarify the nature of the conflict between the request and our standards and to propose alternatives that are consistent with our standards. If such a conflict cannot be resolved, we should terminate the relationship.

The preamble of the AAA Principles recognizes that making "choices among apparently incompatible values" is of the essence of practicing anthropology. But it also emphasizes that "anticipating" and properly "resolving such difficulties is the anthropologist's most fundamental responsibility" (American Anthropological Association 1971). The law has the teeth of sanctions. It uses those sanctions to impose a vision of ethical practice which may be in whole or part incompatible with the practitioner's. It is prudent to engage in some deep and calculated ethical soul-searching before signing on as an expert.

Who (or What) is an Expert?

The term "expertise" clashes with the vocabulary of studied naivete that characterizes anthropological research. Anthropologists tend to equate expertise with that holistic, unerring, and interpretive understanding considered the ideal of fieldwork. Fortunately, "expert," as a legal term of art, has a more modest and pragmatic meaning.

Federal Rule of Evidence 702 defines an expert witness as: "[someone] qualified . . . by knowledge, skill, experience, training or education . . . [to] . . . assist the trier of fact to understand the evidence or determine a fact in issue."

The phrase "qualified by education or experience" normally connotes some combination of training, experience, and ongoing involvement with the field. Although it need not be formal (a retired state trooper, for example, may qualify as an expert at determining a vehicle's speed from the skid marks it leaves on the interstate) the educational level should be that usual in the field (in anthropology, an M.A. or Ph.D.).

Since the linchpin of legal expertise is practiced interpretive skill (the *expert* gives an *opinion* on the meaning of *facts* related by the *eye witness*), an anthropologist is legally an expert because of a trained capability in interpreting cultural behavior.

Federal Rule of Evidence 703 and equivalent state rules allow expert witnesses to form opinions from any type of data, provided that it is of the type normally used in the expert's field. Anthropology is unique for its disciplinary emphasis on in-depth fieldwork; the amount and type of data on which an anthropologist can "reasonably rely" is at the anthropologist's professional discretion.

How Does an Anthropologist Become Qualified as an Expert in a Particular Case?

Before expert testimony can be admitted into evidence, the witness must be qualified as an expert. Opposing counsel may stipulate to your expertise to avoid parading your stellar credentials before judge and jury. If not, testimony will begin with a standardized direct and cross-examination on your resume (which may also be admitted into evidence).

Your counsil will ask several straightforward questions about your education, your research, and your publications. You will also be asked whether you were provided with any information about the facts of the case, or in what way (such as fieldwork) you got the information on which you will base your expert opinions, and whether this type of information is usually relied on by anthropologists. Since most lawyers do not understand what anthropologists do, educate your counsel beforehand and mutually decide whether any particular facts of your background should be emphasized.

Someone will ask if you have previously testified as an expert in similar cases. If you have, your counsel will ask. If you haven't, opposing counsel will ask. After you have testified several times, opposing counsel is unlikely to probe your expertise except in a perfunctory fashion. Among litigation's many ironies, you become an expert by testifying as an expert. The more you testify, the less likely a trial or appellate court will be to find you unqualified.

Opposing counsel will try, with varying degrees of sophistication, to challenge your expert standing. If cross-examining counsel insinuates that anthropologists usually work with monkeys, old bones, or cannibals, or suggests that you should be replaced by a psychologist, sociologist, or private investigator, keep your cool and lucidly explain what anthropologists do and what they learn from it.

But don't expect ignorance. The rules allow opposing counsel to be notified of the names and qualifications of experts and the gist of the testimony. Opposing counsel can also "discover" (receive a copy of) your resume and any report prepared for the case (see Federal Rule of Civil Procedure 26) and read your books and articles. Questions from a well-prepared lawyer may sound like doctoral orals, especially if anthropologists or other social scientists will be testifying on both sides of the case.

Why Expert Witness Rather than Eyewitness?

Since anthropological testimony is usually based upon the testifying anthropologist's own fieldwork, why does the anthropologist testify as an expert rather than an eyewitness? Because the permissible scope of expert witness testimony is broader in four ways than the testimony of eyewitnesses (lay observers to the events in question).

First, eyewitnesses may testify only to what they themselves have seen. Except for the most commonsensical type of inferences from ordinary observation (Federal Rule of Evidence 70) eyewitnesses may not interpret or analyze events. But the very purpose of expert testimony is to provide a trained opinion on the facts. Confusion arises because anthropologists form their opinions substantially from facts they alone have seen.

Second, an eyewitness may testify only about the specific facts at issue in the trial: what the parties did or what was done to them. Since each case must be adjudged on its own facts, testimony about similar behavior by similar people in similar situations is inadmissible. But, since anthropological analysis consists in finding pattern in the repetition of similar events, such testimony is admissible from the anthropological expert.

Third, an eyewitness may not venture an opinion on the meaning of facts. Take, for example, the case of *People v. Kimura,*[4] which often appears in the literature to illustrate the cultural defense.[5] Mrs. Kimura, a traditional Japanese woman living in California, was deserted by her husband. She chose to save herself and her children from the resulting shame by committing *oyaku-shinju,* Japanese customary parent-child suicide. Passersby saw her walk off the Santa Monica beach into the deep waves with her two children and called for rescue. She was saved but her children drowned. She was indicted for murder. Four thousand Japanese-Americans petitioned to have Mrs. Kimura's indictment changed to the lesser criminal violation used in present day Japan for people who try to perform this type of noble suicide. After defense counsel presented the testimony of six psychologists, the case was plea-bargained to voluntary manslaughter (Rentein 1987–88:18).

Had this case gone to court, the testimony of an eyewitness (Japanese-American or otherwise) might well be restricted to a description of how she had seen Mrs. Kimura walk into the water and push her two children under the waves. She might also be able to testify that Mrs. Kimura had looked frightened, sad, sympathetic, or crazed. By contrast, the anthropological expert could testify to the prevalence and cultural significance of *oyaku-shinju*—its origins, principles, and purposes. The testimony could be poignantly peppered with descriptions of other such suicides which the anthropologist had seen, read about, or been told about.

Fourth, with certain limited exceptions, eyewitnesses may testify only about what they have seen; not about what they have been told. Oral traditions cannot be proved through ordinary eyewitness testimony. Such "told-to" testimony violates the hearsay rule. Federal Rule of Evidence 801(c) states: " 'Hearsay' is a statement, other than one made by the declarant while testifying at the trial or hearing, offered in evidence to prove the truth of the matter asserted."

The law assumes that such secondhand statements are unreliable because they cannot be tested in the crucible of cross-examination. Only experts are exempt from the hearsay rule. As Federal Rule of Evidence 703 explains:

> The facts or data in the particular case upon which an expert bases an opinion or inference may be those perceived by or made known to him at or before the hearing. If of a type reasonably relied upon by experts in the particular field in forming opinions or inferences upon the subject, the facts or data need not be admissible in evidence.

Since anthropologists particularly rely on informants' narratives to interpret events, and routinely construct oral histories during fieldwork, "told-to" testimony is of the very essence of anthropological data. For example, consider a hypothetical small rural community whose members have lived for generations without written title or recorded deed to their lands. A real estate developer now wants to build a retirement community on the land and various litigation regarding ownership has arisen.

Testimony by the parties themselves that "My grandfather told me that he bought the land from So and So"; or "My mother explained to me that the boundaries of the property have always been marked by a jagged border of fieldstones"; or "Old Mr. Jones told me that the land by the lake where Ms. Smith lives is really owned by his brother who lent Ms. Smith a space to build a house" violate the hearsay rule. They may not be admitted into evidence by eyewitnesses for the truth they assert.

But an anthropologist who has conducted an ethnography of the community, with the usual compilation of kinship charts and oral histories, may give expert testimony as to both who has rights in the land and the system by which land records are orally kept, land transferred, and land boundaries demarcated in the community. Ascertaining ownership and usufructary rights in land and the underlying juridical rules through oral statements is a traditional anthropological research method.

Curiously, courts have ruled that once an expert has rendered an opinion based on inadmissible hearsay, the jury may even get to hear the hearsay—along with the cautionary instruction that it is "admitted solely to illustrate and explain the expert's opinion" and not for its own truth (American Bar Association Section on Litigation 1983:209).

What Kind of Testimony Should an Anthropological Expert Give?

Theory of the Case

Expert testimony is most successful when there is an understanding between the attorney and the anthropologist on the theory of the case—that is, the way facts will be introduced to prove some point of law. Every legal issue, whether a claim (cause of action) or a defense is composed of elements (conceptual conclusions) each of which must be proved by specific facts. For example, proof of first degree murder requires a killing and a particular mental state *(mens rea),* for example, malice. In the *Kimura* case, the attorney and anthropologist might want to prove that Mrs. Kimura lacked the *mens rea* for first degree murder. She was not malicious. She did not intend to kill her children but to rescue them from enduring shame.

Reaching this understanding takes some mutual education between attorneys and anthropologists. For example, at the outset a lawyer might have some very stereotyped notions about Japanese partiality for suicide and an anthropologist might believe that testifying that *oyaku-shinju* was a widespread cultural trait would provide a sufficient defense. Anthropologist and attorney must work together to find a theory of the case by which undistorted anthropological data fill the factual slots necessary for proof of the elements of a cause of action.

Information sharing is almost always helpful, even when background cultural information has to be forced down the throat of a reluctant harried lawyer. Once anthropologists understand the types of facts needed to prove various legal claims they may assist counsel in finding witnesses, discovering documents, and developing strategies. Strategic brainstorming during trial preparation is important.

The attorney should share with you as many of the facts and as much of the documentation as is compatible with your role in the case. Your assistance as "cultural translator" may be invaluable in helping the eyewitnesses and the attorneys to develop their testimony. Evans and Scott (1983:154), two sociologists who have testified extensively in civil rights and obscenity cases, recommend thorough immersion in the lawyer's files before beginning work. But this has an important limitation. As discussed fully in the Wright article, a testifying witness may be forced to state facts or produce documents adverse to her client's interest, which a behind-the-scenes consultant need not. You and the attorney should decide as early as possible in the case whether your role will be that of an expert witness or a consultant and researcher.

Beware Legal and Anthropological Terms of Art

In law and in anthropology ordinary sounding words are often "terms of art" with specialized meanings. Basic terms such as "community," "race," "minority," "subjective," and "objective" mean vastly different things. The law works with its own vocabulary, and you should not confuse the obligation to be honest about, and honest to, the theoretical bases of your testimony with a compulsion to critique the theoretical soundness of legal testimony. As Evans and Scott properly warn, "Social scientists may go off on their own to do masterful research from their respective professional perspective, yet completely miss the relevant legal questions that must be addressed in court" (1983:154).

The first bastion of anthropological expert testimony was the Indian Claims Commission. Established in 1946 to hear Native American claims against the government based on treaty violations or less than "fair and honorable dealings"[6] the Commission became a natural forum for establishing the dispositive legal import of anthropological research. Under the statute, only a "tribe, band or identifiable group" has standing to sue. As a matter of practice, in order to prove the existence of a group, plaintiffs have to show "that the group exclusively occupied a definite territory for a long period of time" (Rosen 1977:566).

In land claims litigation, the explanation, interpretation, and reconstruction of traditional social and territorial organization, through the testimony for both sides of dozens of honest, competent anthropologists has been essential. Yet, as Rosen observes, "the categories of law or judicial reasoning were not always very appropriate to scholarly inquiry" (1977:566) and "the legal meanings of such terms as 'tribe' and 'band' were so peculiar to many anthropologists" (1977:567) that cases hinged on the inferential consequences of terminological niceties. Legal requirements stimulated a theoretical reformulation of concepts of Native American social structure and property.[7]

In law, words of classification do a fundamentally different kind of work than they do in anthropology. United States law is singularly definitional. The opening paragraphs of a statute, like that of the Indian Land Claims Commission Act, typically contain a series of definitions specifying which persons, entities, and acts are covered by the statute. The purpose of the definition is not to explore or explain social processes. It is to delimit persons or groups which may obtain rights and benefits or be subject to liabilities and penalties under the statute. Attorneys recognize that these labels are arbitrary and flexible; not necessarily congruent with real categories of people. They also recognize that they are powerful and use them as weapons. To keep people out of the statute they argue that the "plain language" (literal meaning) of the statute should control. To bring people under the statute they argue that the "intent" and purpose of the statute should prevail.

Anthropological expert testimony is heard not only in the Court of Claims but in the rougher atmosphere of state and federal trial courts, regulatory hearings, and family and criminal proceedings. Here the terms of art include such words of common parlance as race, culture, minority, ethnicity, parent, family, and community—all of which are currently debated hotly by anthropologists. Experts must remember that litigation is the coercive end of this discourse. Testifying in a case is far different from lobbying, formulating policy, or giving congressional testimony. In these types of testimony anthropological theory can influence broad juridical principles, and abstract debate is appropriate. When testifying in a case, the anthropologist is a part of the evidence (Steward 1955:300–301). Real people win or lose. Expert witnesses need to understand that the ultimate issue on which they testify is how the parties to the case should be treated under the terms of the law by its plain language and penumbra of intent, and that their testimony will be assessed in accordance with the established legal definitions of the concepts.

Concrete Facts and Anecdotes

Under Federal Rule of Evidence 702, an expert may testify "in the form of an opinion or otherwise." The words "or otherwise" in Rule 702 indicate that an expert need not offer an opinion when called to testify. Rather, the expert might provide "factual data or give the jury background material in a technical area" (American Bar Association Section on Litigation

1983:202). Rule 702 allows one to testify as an expert when "specialized knowledge," such as information about a culture, will assist the trier of fact. Although qualification as an expert rests primarily on proven analytical skills, the best anthropological testimony emphasizes concrete facts and examples. There are four reasons for this.

First, legal proof is actually a form of persuasion in which the various pieces of evidence are intuitively weighed by the trier of fact. Graphic stories make strong emotional impressions on both lay jurors and judges who "have heard it all before." Stories are more exciting, better remembered, and easier to understand than statistics or abstractions. In one famous case, an anthropologist was testifying as an expert witness for one side; a sociologist was testifying as an expert witness for the other. The anthropologist's evidence was anecdotal; the sociologist's statistical. The party with the anthropological expert, worried about the impact of the sociologist's "hard" data, made a pretrial motion (a formal request to the court) to limit the sociologist's testimony to narrative material. The side with the anthropological expert lost the motion but won the case. The anthropologist's wrenching tale was more persuasive than the sociologist's calculations.

Second, anthropological abstractions and theories present special evidentiary pitfalls. When admissible, they are turgid and often boring to the uninitiated. Often they are not admissible. The legal standard for admitting an expert's theoretical testimony, the *Frye* test, is that the theory be generally accepted by experts in the field. *United States v. Frye,*[8] decided in 1923, concerned the use of lie detector tests to prove guilt. The court determined that they could not be admitted because the theory that lying caused a measurable change in blood pressure was not then generally accepted.

Frye and its progeny make sense where technical innovation and natural science theory are involved. But the nature of intellectual debate in anthropology makes satisfaction of the *Frye* test a practical impossibility. Any conceptual abstractions are subject to challenge by your adversaries. To an extent *Frye* is on the wane in favor of admitting any expert testimony that will "assist" the trier of fact (Federal Rule of Evidence 702) and is "reasonably relied upon" by the expert (see American Bar Association Section on Litigation 1983:200, 205–206). Some courts have limited *Frye* to technical innovations. But *Frye*-type analysis resurfaces whenever a new scientific technique or controversial theory hits the courts and is a strong weapon for the opposing counsel.

Third, litigating a case should be like directing a drama with the tightness of a theorem. A rule of thumb is that facts and ideas extraneous to proof of the issues should not be introduced. Almost any anthropological abstraction is extraneous. Consider the *Kimura* case again. An anthropologist might testify that in Japanese culture such an act is a socially approved way to spare one's children from public disgrace. From such testimony, the attorney could argue and the jury conclude that the mother lacked malice, an element of the crime of first degree murder.

Now, what if the anthropologist had testified instead that the woman's act was a form of "altruistic suicide," a characteristic of a "shame society" or some other such abstraction? First the characterization would be subject to the *Frye* test; second, the anthropologist would have to explain the concept; and third, it would introduce an unnecessary intermediate step in drawing the legal conclusion. It would now be necessary to find that Mrs. Kimura's drowning of herself and her children was a form of altruistic suicide; therefore, the mother lacked malice, an element of murder in the first degree.[9] Avoid anthropological jargon and leave the lawyers to work their own terms of art into the proof of the case.

Fourth, there is a natural congruence between the anthropological explanation of cultural principles through the compilation, comparison, and distillation of discrete events, and the common law method of legal reasoning by which the facts of the ongoing case are analogized to and distinguished from the facts of similar cases to determine the correct application of legal principles. By testifying about examples of conduct similar to the plaintiff's or defendant's in the culture from which she comes, the anthropological expert can "stretch" the existing precedents and introduce an awareness of pluralism to the court's decision making.

Fifth, introduction of the metalanguage of anthropological theory obfuscates what is often the expert's main job: *cultural translation* directly from the client's culture to terms comprehensible to the judge and jury (Paine 1985:xiii).[10] Triloki N. Pandey beautifully explains how he accomplished such cultural translation through his expert testimony in the Zuni land claims case:

> At the Zuni land claims case in 1981 we had depositions from twelve Zuni elders—but the judge quickly dismissed them: he could not really understand why these tribal leaders were brought to the court or what the significance could be of what they were telling the court. . . .
>
> I suggested that what in a literate society maps and charts and documents do, in a non-literate society, like the Zuni, sacred shrines, centres of pilgrimage, and other sacred cultural markers do. I tried to impress on the court that the latter *are* Zuni charts, and *are* Zuni documents. They are valued as such by the Zuni and that's why Zuni have to visit these places. I pointed out that only a fragment of the Zuni experience has filtered through the various kinds of records compiled by scholars. [Paine 1985:171–172; emphasis in original]

What About Confidentiality Issues?

Anthropologists considering testifying in court are properly concerned about protecting the privacy of their fieldnotes and the identities and confidentialities of their informants. In many field situations, anthropologists routinely and rightly assure informants that their identities and information will be kept confidential. In structured research settings, such a pledge of confidentiality may be a condition of obtaining a subject's signature on a human-subjects consent form. Similarly, information important to an immigration or political asylum case may be dangerous to people still in the home country.

Sometimes crosscutting allegiances may make the situation even more complex. Suppose, for example, an anthropologist has conducted a mental health and social services needs assessment in a town following a massive explosion in a chemical plant that has been the town's major employer. The anthropologist has given the usual assurances of confidentiality to all informants, some of whom could be easily recognized in the anthropologist's fieldnotes. Now, some but not all of those informants have joined in a class action against the chemical corporation and the anthropologist's field data have been subpoenaed by both sides.

The anthropologist, believing his data is too sensitive to release, hires an attorney to quash the subpoena. What if he cannot convince the court of the data's sensitivity? When the court orders disclosure, the anthropologist, whether intending to testify or not, is legally obligated to comply or suffer punishment for contempt—a punishment which may include time spent in jail. Although the pledge of confidentiality may be personally, ethically, and professionally binding, it has no legal significance. The anthropologist, similar to the journalist who will not disclose sources, faces a hard choice. Paragraph 2 of the NAPA Guidelines imposes an obligation to inform "resource persons" and "research subjects" of "our commitment to the principle of confidentiality and of the steps we will take to insure confidentiality. . . . [We should] thoroughly investigate and understand all limitations on our claims of confidentiality and disclosure." Choosing jail time over squealing may be a moral imperative, but on a recurring basis it is a tough way to make a living. Anthropologists should have a working sense of the legal rules and parameters governing the discovery and disclosure of data.

Why Doesn't an Anthropologist's Assurance of Confidentiality Protect an Informant?

> *Privilege* . . . a legal term of art . . . refers to the protection from disclosure which the . . . law . . . affords particular communications in order to promote relationships to which confidentiality of communication is essential. [Shreve and Raven-Hansen 1989:272]

Although confidentiality is essential to anthropological communications, the law has not yet extended the privilege generally accorded to attorney-client, doctor-patient, priest-penitent, and husband-wife communications to include either an anthropologist-informant or a researcher-subject privilege.

Under certain limited circumstances, where the anthropologist "stands in the shoes" of the attorney, the attorney-client privilege may be extended to the anthropologist. Despite some differences among jurisdictions (Federal Rule of Evidence 501 says privilege "shall be governed by the principles of the common law" or where appropriate "in accordance with State law"), the commonalities prevail. Significantly, the privilege attaches only where the client has already consulted legally with the attorney and where confidentiality has not been destroyed by the presence of an outsider.

It covers the anthropologist only where the anthropologist has been hired (or perhaps is under hiring consideration) as a case expert or consultant, and the anthropologist is present at an attorney-client consultation or (perhaps) meets independently with the client for purposes of the case. It covers only communications from the client to the anthropologist, subsequent to and within the scope of the professional litigation relationship. Finally, although it is one of the oldest and most absolute of privileges, it too can be trumped by court order. Obviously, its usefulness for the protection of anthropological confidences from court or public purview is minimal.

Must an Anthropologist Tell Everything? The Scope of Discovery

Happily, there are some protections built into the Federal Rules of Evidence and Civil Procedure. Most govern *discovery*—the pretrial period during which adversaries learn about each other's cases through the ritualized exchange of documents and the interview of parties and witnesses under oath (known as taking depositions).

More information can be exchanged during discovery than can be used at trial. Federal Rule of Civil Procedure 26(b)(1) allows for the discovery of any information that "appears reasonably calculated to lead to the discovery of admissible evidence" and which is "relevant to the subject matter involved in the pending action." The rationale is that pretrial preparation is like pouring a fight down a funnel. By exchanging information in hostile abundance, the issues for trial are narrowed and sharpened. During discovery the touchstone is fairness to the parties and their attorneys—implicitly conceived as regulating the balance of power to protect the adversarial system.

The scope of discovery from an expert witness must strike a balance between one counsel's proprietary/privacy right to her expert's work on the case without intellectual freeloading by adversary counsel, and the other counsel's need for sufficient information to conduct a meaningful cross-examination in the interests of adversarial justice. The Notes of the Advisory Committee on the Federal Rules state:[11]

> Effective cross-examination of an expert witness requires advance preparation. The lawyer even with the help of his own experts frequently cannot anticipate the particular approach his adversary's expert will take or the data on which he will base his judgment on the stand. . . . Similarly, effective rebuttal requires advanced knowledge of the line of testimony on the other side. If the

> latter is foreclosed by a rule against discovery, then the narrowing of issues and elimination of surprise which discovery normally produces are frustrated. . . . Past judicial restrictions on discovery of an adversary's expert, particularly as to his opinions, reflect the fear that one side will benefit unduly from the other's better preparation. The procedure established . . . holds the risk to a minimum.

The expert is deemed a partisan mercenary whose independent need (if acknowledged at all) must be made known specially to the court. The Federal Rules view the attorney as a zealous advocate and the expert witness as a bought brain.

From the point of view of the anthropological expert, the balancing test employed by the courts in determining the scope of discovery means three things. First, you will have to disclose more information if you are to testify at trial than if you are only a behind-the-scenes consulting expert. Second, you are most likely to be made to disclose documents prepared or data collected specifically for the case or related directly to the contested issues (such as your observation of pesticide spraying while conducting prior unrelated fieldwork on the family structure of migrant workers). Third, any privacy or confidentiality concerns you have concerning your data that differ from those of the parties and their attorneys may well be ignored by the court.

Enduring Depositions

Federal Rule of Civil Procedure 26(b)(4) permits broad discovery of "facts known" and "opinions held" by experts who will testify at trial. Such discovery is limited to facts and opinions "acquired or developed in anticipation of litigation or for trial."

The rules establish a sequence for the exchange of expert discovery (Federal Rule of Civil Procedure 26[b][4][A][I]). First, through interrogatories (sworn questionnaires) one party may request the other to state the name of the expert and the subject matter, substance and facts, opinions and grounds for opinions of the expert's testimony. The court may then order further discovery. In practice, however, the sequence is honored in the breach and adverse parties liberally exchange experts' reports with one another and subject one another's experts to lengthy depositions (Graham 1977:172).

In important cases, deposition practice can subject you to long emotionally draining days that can feel like doctoral orals before a politically divided faculty. Evans and Scott caution:

> The social scientists should discuss possible exposure through depositions or interrogatories and must be aware that . . . [their] . . . work and thoughts on the case are subject to examination and scrutiny in this adversarial setting. . . . The social scientist should also be aware that he may be deposed. . . . Sometimes such depositions last for days, inquiring into the most

minute details of preparation and the personal background of the witness. [Evans and Scott 1983:184–85, 198]

Despite the ostensible limitations of the rules, depositions may penetrate far more deeply into background field experience. Your attorney can object to irrelevant questions or "direct" you not to answer them (although deposing counsel often agree that the only objection during a deposition will be to the technical form of the question). Unfortunately, most lawyers are alert only to questions which may be damaging to the case and are unaware of the sensitivities of field research. They may regard your answers to such questions as a mere background travelog.

If you have any hesitancy whatever about answering any deposition question, stop and consult privately with the attorney. The worst possible result will be a nasty statement by opposing counsel to the court reporter: "Let the record reflect that the witness consulted with counsel before answering the question."

Further, discovery information also constitutes a tactical weapon in the litigation war. Although superficially it appears to be a mere formalized exchange of information, statements made by a deponent are admissions under oath and can be used at trial. Contradictions or apparent contradictions between statements made at a deposition and statements made during trial (called "prior inconsistent statements") may be used by opposing counsel during cross-examination to raise doubts about your credibility, reliability, and trustworthiness. Innocent explanatory statements about subtle differences in academic approach and interpretation (which opposing counsel may elicit and encourage with a facade of eager fascination familiar from fieldwork) may be used upon cross-examination to show that your explanation is shaky within the discipline of anthropology or that under the *Frye* test it is inadmissible altogether. Treat deposition testimony with the same seriousness as courtroom testimony and read and correct all deposition transcripts before signing them.

If you are charging a fee for being an expert witness, build the difficulties of deposition testimony into your fee structure without pangs of guilt. Federal Rule of Civil Procedure 26(b)(4)(C) provides for passage of a chunk of this cost onto your client's adversaries. It proclaims that "Unless manifest injustice would result . . . the court shall require that the party seeking discovery pay the expert a reasonable fee for time spent in responding to discovery."

Discovery and the Nontestifying Expert: What is "Work Product"?

An expert who is hired only for behind-the-scenes consulting need not disclose as much as the testifying expert: with the need for discovery to prepare effective cross-examination eliminated, the expert's attorney's proprietary and privacy interests predominate.

Federal Rule of Civil Procedure 26(b)(3) brings anthropologists who act as nontestifying consultants directly under its protection. The rule covers a party's representatives, including "attorney, consultant, surety, indemnitor, insurer, or agent." The rule is best understood as an extension of the attorney's right to protect his "work product." "Work products" are documents and materials containing or revealing ideas, analyses, and theories about the case and its components. The work product doctrine derives from the case of *Hickman v. Taylor,*[12] where the United States Supreme Court reasoned that "Proper preparation . . . demands that . . . [the attorney] . . . assemble information, sift what he considers to be relevant from the irrelevant facts, prepare his legal theories and plan his strategy without undue and needless interference." As incorporated in Federal Rule of Civil Procedure 26(b)(3) the work product rule states in pertinent part:

> [A] party may obtain discovery of documents and tangible things . . . prepared in anticipation of litigation or for trial . . . only upon a showing that the party seeking discovery has substantial need of the materials in the preparation of the party's case and that the party is unable without undue hardship to obtain the substantial equivalent of the materials by other means. In ordering discovery of such materials when the required showing has been made, the court shall protect against disclosure of mental impressions, conclusions, opinions, or legal theories.

As explained in the Notes of the Advisory Committee, when work products are primarily factual, adversary counsel must show that the documents are very important to her case ("substantial need") and virtually impossible to get from other sources ("undue hardship"). When the work product is predominantly analytical ("opinion work product"), the United States Supreme Court indicated in *Upjohn Co. v. United States*[13] that "special protection" is required, and even more than substantial need and undue hardship must be shown. "When factual and opinion work product are intermixed, a court can often protect the latter by inspecting materials *in camera* [out of the presence of counsel seeking discovery] and ordering disclosure only of segregable factual materials" (Shreve and Raven-Hansen 1989:281). Some documents (for example a kinship chart or a reconstruction of a residence pattern) are both. But the court is likely to deem analytical those documents which are directly related to the litigation strategy of the case.

In *Rincon Band v. United States,*[14] the Court of Claims relied in part on the work product rule in denying discovery of documents that the defendant's anthropologist had collected and organized from archival materials. Plaintiffs had sued the United States for failure to protect their water rights from infringement by non–Native Americans; the case turned on the history of agriculture and water development in the reservation area. Plaintiffs had also engaged an anthropologist, who had collected 5,000 pages of relevant documents over a ten-year period. Believing that significant gaps existed in their own experts' documentary records and that some relevant documents no longer existed, plaintiffs sought discovery of records (regardless of whether they would be used at trial), from defendant's anthropologist as the fastest, most certain, and least expensive way to make their documentary record. The court of claims held (partly because the documents were available in public archives) that plaintiffs had failed to show substantial need and undue hardship.

Equal or greater protection is provided under Federal Rule of Civil Procedure 26(b)(4)(B), which provides that discovery may be had by an expert

> who has been retained or specially employed . . . in anticipation of litigation and who is not expected to be called as a witness at trial only . . . upon a showing of exceptional circumstances under which it is impracticable for the party seeking disclosure to obtain facts or opinions on the same subject by other means.

The party seeking discovery must show that the expert has a unique opportunity for firsthand analysis of the facts or is a one-of-a-kind expert. An anthropologist who is the only person to have done longterm research on a people or community at issue may well be such a unique resource.

Adversary counsel may also make a request for the production of documents, or serve a *subpoena duces tecum* (documentary subpoena) upon you or your party. Pursuant to Federal Rule of Civil Procedure 34(a) "Any party may serve on any other party a request . . . to produce and permit the party making the request . . . to inspect and copy, any designated documents (including writings, drawings, graphs, charts, photographs, phono-records, and other data compilations from which information can be obtained . . .)." Document discovery requests and *subpoenas duces tecum* are often drafted as "fishing expeditions," naming every form of information storage from maps and charts to fieldnotes, floppy disks, and *quipus* on anything of remote relationship to the case. While compliance with a subpoena is obligatory, the Federal Rules require general standards of relevance and Rule 34(b) requires that "The request shall set forth the items to be inspected either by individual item or by category, and describe each item with reasonable particularity." The scope of document discovery is a favorite litigation battleground. Typically the documents produced are a mere fraction of those requested. You should inform your attorney about any documents you consider highly sensitive or confidential.

Discovery Rules in Criminal Cases

The rules of criminal procedure permit narrower discovery, reflecting a closer-to-the-chest concern with defendant's rights and a more adversarial tilt. As summarized by Michael J. Saks for the benefit of experts:

> The rules of criminal procedure reflect still other concerns and a different balance to accommodate those concerns. These include protection of a defendant's constitutional rights against disclosing anything that may be incrimina-

> ting, concern that criminal defendants who learn the details of the case against them will combat that evidence with false testimony or threaten witnesses with harm. The solution of the federal rules is a process of defense controlled mutuality (tit for tat exchange of information). Any time the defense seeks discovery of prosecution evidence, the prosecution is entitled to obtain comparable information from the defense. Information that is subject to discovery includes "reports of physical or mental examinations, and of scientific tests or experiments [Federal Rule of Criminal Procedure 16(a)(1)(D) and 16(b)(1)(B)]. But not subject to discovery are "reports, memoranda, or other external . . . documents made by the [defendant, defense counsel, or prosecutor] . . . or by government or defense witnesses [Federal Rule of Criminal Procedure 16(a)(2) and 16(b)(2)]. Thus, the rules of criminal procedure shield more evidence from discovery than the civil rules do, suggesting a more adversarial approach. [1990:307–308]

What about Confidential Data? The Role of Protective Orders

When an anthropologist conducts research for purposes of a specific case, any document or tangible thing discovered or created is reasonably considered work product and is covered by one or more of the provisions discussed above. Researchers should take special precautions, appropriate to their research design, to insure informant confidentiality where necessary, and may also want to advise informants of the context in which the research is being conducted.

More often, however, an anthropologist is called in as an expert because he or she is a known authority on a culture, people, or ethnic group and has many years of prior research experience, reams of unpublished fieldnotes, and scores of stored human secrets. Since these masses of information have been accumulated prior to anyone's intent to litigate they fall outside of the paradigm of proprietary trial preparation versus effective adversarial justice and are subject to a different, more diffuse, test: the balance of relevance against improper intrusion.

The Notes of the Advisory Committee specify that Federal Rule of Civil Procedure 26 "does not address itself to the expert whose information was not acquired in preparation for trial but rather because he was an actor or viewer with respect to transactions or occurrences that are part of the subject matter of the lawsuit."

This category covers, among others, physicians who provide emergency medical care after an automobile accident. It reasonably applies to anthropologists who have witnessed politically motivated violence, cultural adoptions, or land use patterns in the course of prior fieldwork. The advisory committee note explains that such an expert is to "be treated as an ordinary witness." Information, written or not, is discoverable from such a witness within the broad bounds of relevancy stated in Federal Rule of Civil Procedure 26(b)(1): that is, relevant to the subject matter of the action, and admissible or reasonably calculated to lead to the discovery of admissible evidence.

If an anthropologist has actually witnessed or recorded portions of the disputed incident or case subject matter, both oral testimony and documents (including fieldnotes) are discoverable. You may be in a clear conflict between assurances of confidentiality to informants and a court order of disclosure. Fieldnotes or records which relate in a more general way may be undiscoverable as irrelevant.

Where a confidentiality conflict arises, Federal Rule of Civil Procedure 26(c) permits *protective orders.* These are orders of court that limit what one person may get from or do to another. Through a protective order, the court can prevent inquiry into certain matters or documents, limit the extent and scope of that inquiry, or insure that the information will only be disclosed in a certain way, only to certain people, or only to the court.

The Rule 26 protective order provision specially allows a "person from whom discovery is sought" to make a motion "to protect a party or person from annoyance, embarrassment, oppression or undue burden or expense." It covers the privacy concerns of expert witnesses and their informants. The privacy of informants, especially those who may be in politically dangerous situations or involved in competing litigation, can be addressed by protective orders. Similarly, a researcher's assurances of confidentiality may weigh in the balance.

You must be aware, however, that obtaining a protective order is not automatic. Your attorney must make a special written request of the court, which will undoubtedly be strenuously opposed by the other side. Equitable considerations enter into the balance. Thus, a court might look favorably on a motion for a protective order in a political asylum case where an anthropologist had a legitimate concern that disclosure of information would subject informants in the home country to persecution but look askance on a protective order in a Native American land claims case where the expert was concerned about protecting data for fear of triggering interpersonal disputes about land usage.[15]

Protective orders in favor of one's client's adversaries may place burdens on an anthropologist who undertakes research for purposes of the case but hopes to use the data for scholarly purposes as well. Evans and Scott lament that "[w]orking under a protective order restricts the use of the data. The data may not be used in publications or for any other purpose except preparing for court testimony" (1983:198–199).

Seeking a protective order increases litigation costs; and, if a protective order is denied and disclosure is ordered, failure to comply can seriously damage your client's case. Sanctions may be imposed on all concerned and the court may prohibit any litigation of the issues relevant to which discovery is sought. Do not count on a protective order.

Surviving the Witness Stand

Depending on the formality of the court in which you are to testify, it may or may not look like everything you've seen on television from *Perry*

Mason to *L.A. Law*. But TV viewing no more simulates the real thing than reading ethnographies eliminates the culture shock of the opening moments of fieldwork. If you're not used to hanging around courthouses visit the one where you are to testify and do some anthropology. Walk into a courtroom and sit through a trial or a substantial chunk of one. If the trial is not sensational, you will probably be the only spectator. But trials are public by constitutional mandate and we anthropologists are immune to suffering embarrassment from staring at other people doing their thing. Get a sense of the way direct and cross-examinations are conducted and try to hear the examination of an expert witness. You will probably not be able to sit in on any part of the trial in which you testify (except after it is certain that you will be giving no further testimony) since opposing counsel usually want each other's witnesses excluded from the courtroom to prevent their testimony being contaminated by what they have heard others say.

The ritual of the courtroom works. Testifying on the witness stand can be a grueling experience even if you have done it before and you are a natural at public speaking. The adversarial, interrogation-like ambiance disrupts the natural flow of thought and distorts the intended meaning of sentences. (Attorneys learn the art of producing pithy one-liners under pressure through three years of academic drill in the Socratic method. Even then, many do not feel entirely comfortable in the courtroom.)

But preparation and knowing what to expect—if not everything—can substantially improve affect and effect. Prior to trial, you and your attorney should go through one or more practice examinations, with the attorney simulating the style and content of both her direct and the adversary attorney's cross-examination. If you really want to know how you testify, videotape the moot court session (this is what law students do). Also, use the session to continue discussion with the attorney of the best ways to get to say everything you want to say and keep out what you don't want to say. Testimony may be prepared, but it may not be rehearsed. At the actual trial, your attorney will be improvising in part based upon her assessment of what has preceded your testimony and what is likely to follow it. Also, she may forget to ask you something important. Develop an understanding of one another's verbal styles and signals—but don't become so much of a team that you appear to be in "cahoots." The tougher the preparation, the simpler the real thing will be.

On the witness stand, the usual rigid question-and-answer format is generally relaxed for expert witnesses. The court may allow you to testify in "narrative" (expository) style. You may bring notes with you to refresh your recollection. If you are used to speaking from notes you may find them a helpful security blanket; but they should be kept to a minimum for two reasons.

First, eye contact with the judge and/or jury and an apparent total mastery of your subject matter make a better impression. Second—and very important—anything you use in the courtroom before taking the stand or on the stand can be examined by your adversary, used to cross-examine you, and generally introduced into evidence—even if it would be otherwise inadmissible. This applies to a great extent even in criminal trials, where the prosecution generally gets very limited discovery. In federal civil cases, the applicable law is Federal Rule of Evidence 612, which states in part:

> If a witness uses a writing to refresh his memory for the purpose of testifying, either
> (1) while testifying, or
> (2) before testifying, if the court in its discretion determines it is necessary in the interests of justice, an adverse party is entitled to have the writing produced . . . to inspect it, to cross-examine the witness thereon, and to introduce in evidence those portions which relate to the testimony of the witness.

Discuss beforehand with your attorney any notes you intend to bring. Remember that adversary counsel will be literally holding these notes in his hand when he cross-examines you. If he is not thoroughly prepared, the notes may well form the meat of his cross-examination. Any such assistance you provide him should be carefully thought through in advance.

By contrast, the use of "demonstrative evidence" (visual aids) in the form of charts (such as kinship charts), diagrams (e.g., of community organization, land use, or historical changes over time), or maps can make your testimony clearer, more exciting, and more persuasive to judge or jury. Demonstrative evidence can either be prepared in advance or created by you on a chalkboard or marker board made ready for the purpose. Since your attorney probably does not know a kinship chart from a 1040 tax return you must take the lead. If the gist of your testimony consists of tying together the testimony of eyewitnesses into a pattern, practice, or rule of customary law, or if it entails a multifactorial systems analysis (such as reconstructing a land use pattern from archeological, ecological, and oral history data) demonstrative evidence is a must!

Pandey describes his use of such "demonstrative evidence" in the Zuni land claims case:

> By the time we went to court in 1981 we had over eighty thousand "exhibits" in support of the Zuni case: we were a well-prepared team of historians, archaeologists, and anthropologists, but none of our evidence seemed to be getting through to the court. So when I took the stand I saw it as my task to *translate,* to interpret the Zuni vision of life.
>
> I started to treat the court like my classroom and asked whether I could use the blackboard. I then embarked on the telling of the Zuni myth of creation; and I began to plot on the blackboard the inclusive Zuni land area—all this on the basis of what I had learned about their traditions concerning habitation sites, hunting and gathering activities, agriculture and, most important, the sacred sites. Rather to my surprise, the judge started to take an interest

> in what I was saying—and he questioned me for several hours. So I became his informant; . . . I acted as mediator between tribal elders and the judge. [Pandey, quoted in Paine 1985:172; emphasis in original]

Cross-examination (an interrogation designed to destroy your expert testimony, denigrate your credibility, and demean your objectivity) is necessarily a painful experience. Skillful counsel can and will use hypothetical questions and negative interrogative sentences (of the "Have you stopped beating your wife?" variety) to make you look ridiculous. Do not let yourself be forced into retracting a valid point or asserting it with a certainty and inclusiveness the data does not warrant.

There are limits. Cross-examining counsel can generally only ask you questions about things you have talked about on direct examination. The sole exception to this is that under Federal Rule of Evidence 705 if you have not disclosed the facts or data underlying your opinion, you can be required to do so on cross-examination. But this is unlikely to come up in practice because your field research is an important part of what you will probably testify to on direct examination. Further, many states differ from the federal rule in requiring an expert to disclose the underlying facts through discovery or direct examination before testifying.

If a question is improper (or even worrisome) your attorney will object. When you hear him say "Objection, your honor!" stop talking and wait for the judge to rule. If the judge overrules the objection you must answer. But in the intervening split second try to determine the trouble area your attorney was trying to flag. It may be a mere technicality of the way the question was phrased—but it may be a question which requires a carefully worded answer.

If cross-examining counsel is not thoroughly prepared for the examination, you are likely to feel belittled and demeaned by the pettiness and inappropriateness of his jabs. They will probably center around apparent inconsistencies and gaps in your testimony which may be more apparent than real.

If cross-examining counsel is well prepared you are likely to feel scorched and grilled. Expect that adversary counsel or his own consulting expert has read all of your publications and those of other scholars writing on the same subject and may try to force you to defend your views against those of others. If you have published on the subject of your testimony and, with appropriate academic modesty, described your data as incomplete, your conclusions as tentative, your theoretical formulations as preliminary, or your opinions as personal, expect that cross-examining counsel will use your own words to impeach you.

For example, in the Australian case of *Milpirrum v. Nabalco Pty. Ltd. and the Commonwealth of Australia,*[13] an Aboriginal land claim matter, the Solicitor-General cross-examined W. E. H. Stanner on the anthropological debate over whether foraging bands or clan groupings were the fundamental unit in Aboriginal territorial organization; the distinctions between oral tradition and oral testimony; anthropological generalization from informants' statements; discrepancies among maps of the clan territory constructed by different anthropologists; and the certainty or uncertainty of anthropological knowledge (Paine 1985:174).

The best way to avoid such problems is to keep your testimony concrete, clear, and ethnographic, and your manner cool. If cross-examining counsel does succeed in tripping you up by making you say, or seem to say, something you didn't quite mean, your own counsel has a right of redirect examination to let you fill in the gaps and clarify the misunderstandings.

Notes

[1]28 U.S.C. 2072.

[2]One possible approach would be for anthropological organizations to submit *amicus curiae* ("friend of the court") briefs. *Amicus curiae* briefs are usually submitted with permission of the court by organizations, institutions, or interest groups that have an interest in the point of law at issue but no direct interest in the case itself. They are appropriately more abstract, theoretical, and scholarly than most party briefs. A program for the submission of *amicus* briefs which might serve as a model for interested anthropologists has recently been begun collaboratively by the American Psychology Law Society and the American Psychological Association (for a full description see Roesch et al. 1991).

[3]In both anthropology and law, effective advocacy depends on maintaining professional honesty and objectivity. In a major land claims case by the Gitskan and Wet'suwet'en against British Columbia, the British Columbia Supreme Court discounted the pivotal expert testimony of two anthropologists who had done years of participant-observation research, submitted a 691-page report, and testified for ten days. The court found that the anthropologist "did not conduct their investigations in accordance with accepted scientific practices," failed to consider research done by other scholars, "dealt almost exclusively with chiefs . . . [which was] . . . fatal to the credibility and reliability of their conclusions," made propositions "based on facts not proven in evidence," and seemed "to be describing a society" which the court did "not recognize from the evidence of the lay witnesses" (Delgamook v. The Queen, [Sup. Ct of British Columbia, No. 0843 Smithers Registry 1990 44 at 50]). If the court's perception of the testimony is, in fact, accurate, the legal critique was no different from what a scholarly critique would be. If the court's critique is incorrect, the case is an object lesson in the need for an expert to display an appearance of impartiality. Unfortunately, the court was improperly led to believe that the experts' apparent bias resulted from the anthropologists' ethical obligation under Section 1 of the AAA Statement of Ethics, stating "In research, an anthropologist's paramount responsibility is to those he studies." Expert anthropologists should remember, in their zeal to help their people, their obligation to maintain the credibility of anthropology as a profession.

[4]People v. Kimamura, No. A-091133 (Los Angeles Cty. Super. Ct., filed April 24, 1985).

[5]The "cultural defense" permits introduction of cultural factors to mitigate the severity of the crime and sentence. For discussions of *Kimura* in this regard see Rentein (1987–88); Sheybani (1987); and Weinhelman (n.d.).

[6]25 U.S.C. 70.

[7]To get a historical sense of the ongoing dialogue among anthropologists who testified in the land claims cases see Hopper (1990), Lurie (1955, 1956), Manners (1956), Steward (1955), and Stewart (1979).

[8]U.S. v. Frye, 293 F.103 (D.C. Cir. 1923).

[9]One now-famous example of the disservice of anthropological theorizing to anthropological testimony comes from the "battle of the experts" between Julian Steward (testifying for the United States government) and Omer Stewart (testifying for the Northern Paiute) before the Indian Claims Commission. For Steward, grappling with the legal definitions, concepts, and issues was an impetus to developing his own scholarly themes and concepts in regard to band organization and concepts of property (Steward 1955).

Yet, Omer Stewart (with over 25 years of experience as an expert witness) writes that theoretical brilliance and successful expert witness testimony are different things. Between

Julian Stewart, his first professor of anthropology, who "had been certified a genius at about 16, when a national search led to his selection to attend a special school for geniuses" and himself—a mediocre student who spent vacations working on the farm—and "[on] the basis of their reputation among professional anthropologists" there was "no contest" (Stewart 1979:109–110). Stewart continues

> Nevertheless, the Indian Claims Commission awarded the claim to the Northern Paiute, and the Indians won payments in all of the cases in which I testified. . . . I believe . . . that as an expert witness the anthropologist's primary role is the presentation of objective data, with only the addition of expressing his or her opinion based on the data and his or her training as an anthropologist. I could do little but present objective data and base my opinion on the data. Julian, on the other hand, was a great and honored theoretician. From the time of his first publication on the Northern Paiute to his appearance as an expert witness for the Department of Justice in the Northern Paiute case, he had developed new theories. When it was obvious that there were discrepancies between statements in his early publications and those made on the witness stand the attorneys for the Indians asked if Julian would explain the basis for the discrepancies. The answer was, in effect, that Julian had changed his theory. [Stewart 1979:81]

[10]When injudiciously used, even such basic terms as "culture" may sour one's testimony. In Delgamuukw v. The Queen (No. 0843, Smithers Registry 1990 at 44) the British Columbia Supreme Court opined that while "culture, in a generic sense, may have a general role in the formulation of opinions in these sciences [anthropology] . . . where the plaintiffs and their ancestors are the only sources of these histories, the Court may not be the best forum for resolving such difficult and controversial *academic* questions" (emphasis added).

[11]The Advisory Committee is an officially designated committee of judges, attorneys, and legal scholars. The committee's "Notes" to new Federal Rules and amendments to existing rules are published accompanying the rules themselves and are regarded as authoritative statements of the rules' history, purposes, intent, and interpretation.

[12]Hickman v. Taylor, 329 U.S. 495, 498–512 (1947).

[13]Upjohn Co. v. United States, 449 U.S. 383 (1981).

[14]Rincon Band v. United States, No. 80-A, United States Court of Claims (slip opinion filed February 29, 1980).

[15]Barsh's (1986:393) discussion of protective orders requested by a Native American tribe in the course of proceedings before the Federal Energy Regulatory Commission illustrates the way courts balance confidentiality issues. In the course of hearings on the adverse impact to the Kootenai religion from the development of hydroelectric power at Flathead Lake (*Northern Lights, Inc.,* 16 Fed. Energy Reg. Comm'n Rep. [CCH] paragraph 63, 062 [1981]; 19 Fed. Reg. Comm'n Rep [CCH] paragraph 63, 016 (1982); 22 Fed. Energy Reg. Comm'n Rep. [CCH] paragraph 63, 068 [1983]):

> [T]he tribe moved to preclude discovery of:
> (a) the contents of individual and personal visions of Kootenai Indians,
> (b) the details of certain rituals performed for vision quests and other religious ceremonies, and
> (c) the names and functions of spiritual entities in Kootenai religion,
>
> as well as the times and places of ceremonies. The administrative law judge refused to issue a blanket protective order, but ruled that all submissions on these points would remain confidential. The judge, subsequently warned the power company's expert witnesses not to share discovered evidence with others [but later permitted the release of confidential discovered information to the Keeper of the National Register of Historic Places]. Although judges have discretion to examine *in camera* [examination by the judges' eyes alone], or seal the record of sensitive evidence they are likely to give greater weight to the Sixth Amendment requirements of confrontation and public trial. [Barsh 1986:393]

[16]17 Federal Law Reports 141 (1971). The transcript of this cross-examination is reproduced in Paine (1985). For a summary of the legislative changes that followed the Aborigines' loss in this case and for discussion of more recent land claims litigation in Australia, see Maddock (1986).

References Cited

Americas Watch

1987 Americas Watch, The Civilian Toll 1986–1987. Ninth supplement on the Report on Human Rights in El Salvador, vol I. New York: Americas Watch.

1988 Americas Watch, Closing The Space: Human Rights in Guatemala. May 1987–October 1988. New York: Americas Watch

American Anthropological Association

1971 Principles of Professional Responsibility. Adopted by the Council of the American Anthropological Association.

American Bar Association Section on Litigation

1983 Emerging Problems Under the Federal Rules of Evidence. American Bar Association.

Amnesty International

1989 United States of America: The Death Penalty. London: Amnesty International Publications.

Anker, Deborah

1990 Determining Asylum Claims in the United States: Summary Report of an Empirical Study of the Adjudication of Asylum Claims before the Immigration Court. International Journal of Refugee Law 2:252–264.

Barsh, Russel Lawrence

1986 The Illusion of Religious Freedom for Indigenous Americans. Oregon Law Review 65:363–415.

Berman, H.

1977 The Origins of Western Legal Science. Harvard Law Review 90:900–993.

Boas, Franz

1916 Tsimshian Mythology. U.S. Bureau of Ethnology 31st Annual Report. Washington, DC: U.S. Bureau of Ethnology.

Cohen, Julius

1963 The Value of Value Symbols in Law. *In* Essays on Jurisprudence from the Columbia Law Review. New York: Columbia University Press.

Comte, Auguste

1830–42 The Course of Positive Philosophy (Cours de philosophie positive). Paris: Bachelier.

Cranor, Carol, and Kurt Nutting

1990 Law and Philosophy. International Journal for Jurisprudence and Legal Philosophy 9(2):115–156.

De Havenon, Anna Lou

1989–90 Charles Dickens Meets Franz Kafka: The Maladministration of New York City's Public Assistance Programs. New York University Review of Law and Social Change XVII (2):231–254.

Dobyns, Henry F.

1978 Taking the Witness Stand. *In* Applied Anthropology in America. Elisabeth M. Eddy and William L. Partridge, eds. New York: Columbia University Press.

Donahue, Charles, Jr.

1980 The Future of the Concept of Property Predicted from Its Past. *In* Nomos XXII Property. J. R. Pennock and J. W. Chapman, eds. Pp. 28–68. New York: New York University Press.

Durkheim, Emile

1938[1901] The Rules of Sociological Method. Chicago: University of Chicago Press.

Engels, Friedrich

1970[1884] The Origin of the Family, Private Property, and the State. *In* Karl Marx and Friedrich Engels, Selected Works, Vol. III. Moscow: Progress Publishers.

Evans, Sandra S., and Joseph E. Scott
1983 Social Scientists as Expert Witnesses: Their Use, Misuse and Sometimes Abuse. Law and Policy Quarterly 5(2):181–214.
Fagen, P.
1984 Applying for Political Asylum in New York: Law, Policy and Administrative Practice. New York University Occasional Paper no. 41. New York: New York University.
Feinstein, Alvan
1988 Scientific Standards in Epidemiological Studies of the Menace of Daily Life. Science 242:1257–1263.
Frankel, M.
1986 Causation and Lawyers' Causes. Regulatory Toxicology and Pharmacology 6:89–94.
Frazer, James
1890 The Golden Bough. New York: Macmillan.
Friedmann, W.
1967 Legal Theory. 5th edition. New York: Columbia University Press.
Gardner, Robert
1963 Dead Birds. Film Study Center, Peabody Museum, Harvard University, prod. Contemporary Films, Inc., dist. 83 minutes.
Geertz, Clifford
1983 Local Knowledge: Further Essays in Interpretive Anthropology. New York: Basic Books.
1988 Works and Lives: The Anthropologist as Author. Stanford: Stanford University Press.
Graham, Michael H.
1977 Discovery of Experts under Rule 26 (b)(4) of the Federal Rules of Civil Procedure: Part Two. An Empirical Study and a Proposal, University of Illinois Law Forum:169–220.
Gray-Donald, Katherine, and Michael S. Kramer
1988 Causality Inferences in Observational vs. Experimental Studies. American Journal of Epidemiology 127(5):885–892.
Hawkes, Terrence
1977 Structuralism and Semiotics. Berkeley: University of California Press.
Heider, G. K.
1979 Grand Valley Dani: Peaceful Warriors. New York: Holt, Rinehart and Winston.
Hobbes, Thomas
1952[1651] The Leviathan. N. Fuller, ed. Chicago: Brittanica.
Hoebel, E. A., and T. Weaver
1979 Anthropology and the Human Experience. 5th Edition. New York: McGraw-Hill.
Holmes, Louis B.
1986 Letter. Journal of American Medical Association 256(22):3096.
Hopper, Kim
1990 Research Findings as Testimony: A Note of the Ethnographer as Expert Witness. Human Organization 49:110.
Joans, Barbara
1984 Problems in Pocatello: A Study in Linguistic Misunderstanding. Practicing Anthropology 6(3/4):6, 8..
Johnson, F. M., and M. L. Snell
1986 Short Term Tests are Unable to Distinguish between Human and Non-Carcinogens. Cancer Investigation 4(3):271–280.
Journal of the American Medical Association
1986 Letters to the Editor. Journal of the American Medical Association 256(22):3095–3096.
Kairys, David
1982 The Politics of Law: A Progressive Critique. New York: Pantheon Books.
Kalin, Walter
1986 Troubled Communication: Cross-Cultural Misunderstandings in the Asylum Hearing. International Migration Review 20:230–241.
Keeton, L. Page (ed.)
1984 The Law of Torts, 5th Edition. St. Paul: West Publishing.

Kelman, Mark
1987 A Guide to Critical Legal Studies. Cambridge: Harvard University Press.
Kot, Veronika
1988 The Impact of Cultural Factors on Credibility in the Asylum Context. San Francisco: Immigrant Legal Resource Center.
Leach, Edmond
1974 Levi-Strauss. Revised edition. London: Fontana/Collins.
Levi-Strauss, Claude
1974 Triste Tropiques. New York: Atheneum.
Lieberman, J. H.
1988 Meat Fights and Song Duels: Three Professors at Temple University Delve into Some *Very* Alternative Dispute Resolution. Student Lawyer 17(3):47.
Lloyd, Lord of Hampstead, and M. D. A. Freeman
1985 Lloyd's Introduction to Jurisprudence. 5th edition. London: Stevens & Sons.
Logan, Deana Dorman
1989 Is it Mitigation or Aggravation, CACJ Forum Sept/Oct 1989:14.
Loucky, James
1989 Guatemalan Refugees and the Politics of Asylum. Protocol 2(3):1.
Lurie, Nancy Oestreich
1955 Anthropology and Indian Claims Litigation: Problems, Opportunities, and Recommendations. Ethnohistory 2:357.
1956 A Reply to "Land Claim Cases: Anthropologists in Conflict." Ethnohistory 3:72–81.
Maddock, Kenneth
1986 Asking for Utopia: A Study in Aboriginal Land Rights. *In* Anthropology of Law in the Netherlands. von Benda-Beckmann and Strijbosch, eds. Dordrecht: Foris Publications.
Maine, Sir Henry
1905 Ancient Law. London: Routledge.
Malinowski, Bronislaw
1961[1922] Argonauts of the Western Pacific: An Account of Native Enterprise and Adventure in the Archipelagoes of Melanesian New Guinea. New York: E. P. Dutton.
1954[1948] Baloma; the Spirits of the Dead in the Trobriand Islands. *In* Magic, Science and Religion and Other Essays. Garden City, New York: Doubleday Anchor Books.
Mancias, P. T.
1987 A History & Philosophy of the Social Sciences. Oxford: Basil Blackwell.
Manners, Robert A.
1956 The Land Claims Cases: Anthropologists in Conflict. Ethnohistory 3:72–81.
Marcus, G. E., and M. M. Fischer
1986 Anthropology as Cultural Critique: An Experimental Moment in the Human Sciences. Chicago: University of Chicago Press.
Maronpot, et al.
1986 Strain A Mouse Pulmonary Test Results for Chemicals Previously Tested in the National Cancer Institute for Carcinogenity Tests. Journal of the National Cancer Institute 76(6):1101–1112.
McCloskey, Michael, Howard Egeth, and Judith McKenna (eds.)
1986 The Ethics of Expert Testimony. Law and Human Behavior 10(1–2).
McLellan, David
1976 Karl Marx. New York: Penguin Books.
Morgan, Lewis Henry
1870 Systems of Consanguinity and Affinity of the Human Family. Washington, DC: Smithsonian Institution.
1963[1877] Ancient Society. E. Leacock, ed. New York: Meridian Books.
Paine, Robert (ed.)
1985 Anthropology and Advocacy, First Encounters. St. John's, Newfoundland: Institute of Social and Economic Research, Memorial University of Newfoundland.
Patterson, E. W.
1953 Jurisprudence: Men and Ideas of the Law. Brooklyn: Foundation Press.
Radcliffe-Brown, A. R.
1922 The Andaman Islanders. Cambridge: University Press.
1952 Structure and Function in Primitive Society. London: Cohen and West.

Rentein, Alison Dundes
1987–88 Culture and Culpability: A Study of Contrasts. Beverly Hills Bar Association Journal 22(1):17.
Rigby, Peter
1985 Persistent Pastoralists: Nomadic Societies in Transition. London: Zed Books.
1987–88 Pastoralism, Egalitarianism, and the State: The Eastern African Case. Critique of Anthropology 7:17–32.
1992 Cattle, Capitalism, and Class: Ilparakuyo Maasai Transformations. Philadelphia: Temple University Press.
Roesch, Ronald, et al.
1991 Social Science and the Courts: The Role of Amicus Curiae Briefs. Law and Human Behavior 15(1):1–11.
Rosen, Lawrence
1977 The Anthropologist as Expert Witness. American Anthropologist 79:555–578.
1979 Response to Stewart. American Anthropologist 81:111–112.
Saks, Michael J.
1990 Expert Witnesses, Nonexpert Witnesses, and Nonwitness Experts. Law and Human Behavior 14(4):291–313.
Sapir, Edward
1949 Selected Writings in Language Culture and Personality. D. G. Mandelbaum, ed. Berkeley: University of California Press.
Sevareid, Peter
1986 Sex and Witchcraft, An Interdisciplinary, Jointly Taught course in Comparative Dispute Settlement. Third World Legal Studies:79.
Sheybani, Malek-Mithra
1987 Cultural Defense: One Person's Culture is Another's Crime. Loyola Los Angeles International and Comparative Law Journal 9:751–783.
Shreve, Gene, and Peter Raven-Hansen
1989 Understanding Civil Procedure. New York: Matthew Bender.
Sklar, Helen, Bill Ong Hing, and Mark Silverman, eds.
1985 Salvadoran and Guatemalan Asylum Cases: A Practitioner's Guide to Representing Clients in Deportation Proceedings. San Francisco: Immigrants Legal Resource Center.
Small, Ben F.
1985 Gaffing at a Thing Called Cause: Medico-legal Conflicts in the Concept of Causation. Texas Law Review 31:630–659.
Stevens, R.
1983 Law School: Legal Education in America from the 1850s to the 1980s. Chapel Hill: University of North Carolina Press.
Steward, Julian
1955 Theory and Application in Social Science. Ethnohistory 2:292–302.
Stewart, Omer C.
1973 Anthropologists as Expert Witnesses for Indians: Claims and Peyote Cases. *In* Anthropology and the American Indian. Pp. 35–42. San Francisco: Indian Historian Press.
1979 An Expert Witness Answers Rosen. American Anthropologist 81:108–111.
Twinning, William
1982 The Rationalist Tradition of Evidence Scholarship. *In* Well and Truly Tried: Essays on Evidence in Honour of Sir Richard Eggleston. E. Campbell and L. Waller, eds. Pp. 211–234. Sydney: Law Book Company.
1984a Taking Facts Seriously. Journal of Legal Education 34:22.
1984b Evidence and Legal Theory. Modern Law Review 47:261–283.
1985 Theories of Evidence: Bentham and Wigmore. Stanford: Stanford University Press.
Tylor, Sir Edward Burnett
1871 Primitive Culture. London: J. Murray.
Vico, Giambattista
1948[1725] The New Science. T. G. Bergin and M. H. Fisch, trans. Ithaca: Cornell University Press.
Weinhelman, Michael
n.d. The Cultural Defense in Criminal Law.

White, David
1990 Anthropologists, Law and Cultural Resources Management. Paper presented at the Annual Meeting of the Southwest Anthropological Association, Long Beach, CA.

About the Contributors

Lynn Alvarez (J.D., Boalt Hall School of Law) is an attorney with the Immigrants Rights Office, Legal Aid Foundation of Los Angeles. She specializes in the rights of refugees, both children and adults, on both an individual and class basis.

Michael Davidson (M.A., Anthropology, University of Hawaii; M.Ph., Anthropology, Yale University; J.D., Columbia University School of Law) is a partner in the New York law firm of Jacob, Medinger, Finnegan, and Hart, where he specializes in toxic tort litigation. His activities have ranged from research on Pacific peoples to investigation of nursing home abuses.

Randy Frances Kandel (Ph.D., Anthropology, City University of New York; J.D., New York University School of Law) has explored and experienced perspectives on the law-anthropology connection ranging from academic anthropology to law firm litigation practice. She is an associate professor at Loyola Law School, Los Angeles.

James Loucky (Ph.D., Anthropology, University of California at Los Angeles) is an assistant professor in the department of anthropology at Western Washington University. Since the mid 1970s he has conducted extensive research with Latin American peoples and applied anthropology in the interests of human rights.

Peter Rigby (Ph.D., Anthropology, Cambridge University) is a professor of anthropology at Temple University. He was born in India of English parents and received his undergraduate education at Capetown University. He is a citizen of Uganda and has done extensive research on East African societies.

Peter Sevareid (J.D., Georgetown University; L.L.M., Yale University) is a law professor at Temple University. With Rigby he has taught a joint course to law and anthropology students since 1979. He taught for three years in Kenya under Ford Foundation auspices and during that period he edited the *East African Law Journal*. He has done field research in Northern Liberia and is the author of articles on family law and comparative dispute settlements in East and West Africa.

Isabel Wright (Ph.D., Anthropology, University of California, Davis). Wright was raised in Egypt, educated in Wales, and was a long time resident of Canada and the United States. She was, until her tragic death from cancer on June 23, 1991, an expert consultant in capital case litigation in California.